THE UNITED STATES AMONG THE NATIONS

THE UNITED STATES
AMONG
THE NATIONS

LECTURES ARRANGED BY THE
UNIVERSITY OF CALIFORNIA COMMITTEE
ON INTERNATIONAL RELATIONS

◆

FIRST SERIES
DELIVERED AUTUMN 1936

Essay Index Reprint Series

Originally published by:
UNIVERSITY OF CALIFORNIA PRESS

BOOKS FOR LIBRARIES PRESS
FREEPORT, NEW YORK

First Published 1937
Reprinted 1968

LIBRARY OF CONGRESS CATALOG CARD NUMBER:

68-54336

MANUFACTURED
BY
HALLMARK LITHOGRAPHERS, INC.
IN THE U.S.A.

CONTENTS

PREFACE

IN THE WINTER AND SPRING OF 1936, the University of California Committee on International Relations, at the suggestion of President Robert Gordon Sproul, considered in several meetings various means of quickening the interest and broadening the information of students in the University, with reference to international problems and the concern of the United States therewith. One outcome of these discussions was a decision to have a series of lectures in the fall semester which should be open both to the student body and to the general public. For this initial series, the theme selected was "The United States Among the Nations," and it was planned that similar series upon kindred themes should be made an annual event.

The 1936 lectures, as delivered, constitute the present volume. As will be seen, all the writers except one are professors of the University, the exception being Mr. Chester Rowell, editor of the San Francisco *Chronicle* and member of the Board of Regents of the University. Each has written informally as an individual and upon a separate topic. No attempt has been made artificially to harmonize or unify their presentations, or to adopt a precise mode of reference.* Never-

---

* The name America has been here used, as its connotation in the respective lectures will indicate, in the broad inclusive sense of the Western Hemisphere, comprising the twenty-one republics and one dominion of the two American continents; in the still inclusive sense of Pan America, comprising the twenty Latin American republics and the North American republic, the United States of America; and finally in restricted application, with which almost unavoidably it is often used, to the United States alone.

theless, it is hoped that the treatments of the several subjects have been such as to complement and reënforce one another, as well as the central theme of America in the concert of nations.

The lectures were given on Wednesday evenings from September 16 to November 4, 1936. The interest manifested both by the student body and by the citizenry of Berkeley was highly gratifying, the audiences on several occasions exhausting the seating capacity of Wheeler Auditorium. In this published presentation it is hoped that a still wider audience may be reached.

COMMITTEE ON INTERNATIONAL RELATIONS

B. H. CROCHERON, *Chairman*
F. C. STEVENS, *Secretary*
A. C. BLAISDELL
E. D. DICKINSON
J. W. GILMORE
T. H. GOODSPEED
H. F. GRADY
NOEL KEYS
F. D. LESSING
H. I. PRIESTLEY
F. M. RUSSELL
F. H. SWIFT

FROM WASHINGTON TO ROOSEVELT: BASIC FACTORS AND TRADITIONS IN AMERICAN FOREIGN POLICY

———

EUGENE I. MCCORMAC
PROFESSOR OF AMERICAN HISTORY
IN THE UNIVERSITY OF CALIFORNIA

Lecture delivered September 16, 1936

FROM WASHINGTON TO ROOSEVELT: BASIC FACTORS AND TRADITIONS IN AMERICAN FOREIGN POLICY

E ARLY IN 1778, Benjamin Franklin and his colleagues, Silas Deane and Arthur Lee, induced the French monarchy to conclude a treaty of defensive alliance with the new United States. At the time, it was thought to be a signal diplomatic victory for the young nation; and it was, for as soon as it had been signed, the French government openly gave the Americans aid—military, naval, and financial. The treaty and the aid met with the approval of all Americans, for the aid was an important factor in their struggle for independence. After independence had been achieved, however, thoughtful statesmen began to feel that an alliance with any European nation was not an unmixed blessing, because it might involve the United States in European schemes concerned with the "balance of power."

Our obligations under the alliance of 1778 were not put to a real test until after our Constitution had been adopted and General Washington had become President of the United States. In 1789, the revolutionists in France opened Pandora's box, and that country soon became involved in wars with its neighbors. So far as the United States was concerned, the most important of these wars was that with Great Britain, which began in 1795.

At that time, there were two political parties in the United States. One was the Federalist, which possessed control of the government and looked to Alexander Hamilton for guidance. Thomas Jefferson was the accepted leader of the opposition party, which had adopted the name Republican. Generally speaking, the Republicans sympathized with the revolutionists in France, especially during the early stages of their assault on special privileges. The Federalists were inclined to look with disfavor upon the revolution, and when war with Great Britain resulted, their sympathies were with the British rather than the French.

The Washington administration was faced with a difficult problem. On the one hand, the United States was an ally of France under the treaty of 1778; on the other hand, the party in power favored the British; furthermore, it seemed almost suicidal for the new nation to become involved in European warfare. To make matters worse, the new French minister, Citizen Genêt, had arrived and was issuing French commissions to Americans and endeavoring to recruit soldiers.

Much perplexed, Washington consulted his cabinet; and Hamilton, who possessed a fertile brain and a conscience easily adjusted to expediency, propounded a theory which would free the United States from obligations under the treaty of 1778. He maintained that France was engaged in an *offensive* rather than a *defensive* war; in addition, the treaty had been made with the monarchy, and did not bind the Americans to aid the revolutionists. Doubtless this was sophistry, but his theory was accepted by the administration, and the President issued his well-known Neutrality Proclamation.

Washington's proclamation of 1793 was a document of great importance in our diplomatic history. By it, this country abandoned coöperation with European states and adopted a policy of isolation, a policy to which it was to adhere for many years. The neutrality policy announced in the proclamation was a makeshift, but in his farewell address Washington urged it as a general principle which should be followed, because "Europe has a set of primary interests which to us have none or very remote relation." President Adams expressed similar views, and the epitome of Jefferson's foreign policy, as announced in his inaugural address, was "honest friendship with all nations, entangling alliances with none."

In the resolution to refrain from meddling in European affairs, the United States could do as it saw fit; but it was not so easy to compel Europe to respect the wishes and rights of the United States. From as early as 1793 the belligerents had jeopardized American commerce; and during the titanic contest between Napoleon and Great Britain, American ships could not venture upon the high seas without being subject to capture under French decrees or British orders in council. Averse to war, President Jefferson sought a remedy in what he called "peaceable coercion," in other words, a commercial boycott against both belligerents until they had agreed to respect the rights of American shippers. He had advised such a policy, as a substitute for war, at the beginning of his administration,[1] and in 1807, at his suggestion, Congress enacted the embargo law which forbade American vessels to leave their home ports. The remedy proved ineffective, however, and in Madison's administration we engaged in a second war with Great Britain.

---

[1] "Our commerce is so valuable to them, that they will be glad to purchase it, when the only price we ask is to do us justice."—Jefferson to Dr. Logan, March 22, 1801.

The downfall of Napoleon in 1815 removed the cause of interference with neutral commerce, and Americans could turn to the development of their own country; but annoyances from the outside had not been entirely removed. Louisiana had been acquired peaceably by purchase in 1803; but Spanish Florida was troublesome, and there were fears that some strong nation might acquire Cuba and dominate the Gulf of Mexico, and menace our use of the Mississippi. Then, too, there were fears that European powers coöperating under the name "Holy Alliance" might attempt to seize the South American republics, or to restore them to Spain.

President Monroe and his able secretary of state, John Quincy Adams, felt that the time had come when the United States should formulate a definite policy with respect to the affairs of the New World, and should announce that policy to the world. Florida was acquired by treaty in 1819, and in his message of December 2, 1823, Monroe incorporated declarations which have ever since been called the "Monroe Doctrine." Two things, he said, would be considered by the United States as unfriendly and dangerous. These were the establishment of new colonies in America by European nations, or any attempt to impose the European "system" upon any part of the American continents. The first statement is definite, and the second seems purposely to have been made rather vague. Coupled with the principles established by Washington and Jefferson, the Monroe Doctrine amounted to this: We shall keep out of your dooryard, and you must not trespass upon ours. Older books on the subject assume that Americans feared most of all the machinations of the "Holy Alliance" the leading members of which, at that time, were Russia, Austria, and France; but more recent research has disclosed that Great Britain was the only nation which our country really feared. It was the most powerful, and during that period it seemed to have a disposition to curb the growth and development of the United States. To be sure, George Canning, the British foreign secretary, had proposed a joint declaration in respect to Latin America; but in this proposal, Secretary Adams thought he discerned only another scheme of John Bull to prevent the United States from acquiring needed territory—Cuba, for example.

The Panama Congress of 1826 was an interesting sequel to the Monroe Doctrine. Several South American countries decided to hold a congress at Panama for the purpose of discussing American affairs and, possibly, of formulating policies beneficial to both American continents. The United States was invited to send delegates, and President Adams accepted the invitation. When he notified Congress, however, and asked for an appropriation to defray the expenses of the delegation, he received an unexpected rebuff. The Jacksonite majority neglected no opportunity to deal a blow at Adams, and they made the most of this one. By accepting the invitation, they said, the President had usurped the war powers of Congress, violated the Constitution, and made himself a czar. When the storm of invectives had spent itself, they voted the appropriation; but before our delegates reached Panama, the congress had adjourned. The results of this congress were negligible, but they might have been different had the United States been represented and taken a leading part. At least one evil might have been avoided. The lone-hand policy of enforcing the Monroe Doctrine caused the resentment of those whom it was intended to protect. But whatever the results of our active participation at Panama might have been, the fact remains that the President's coöperative program was defeated by personal and partisan animosity.

As years have passed, the Monroe Doctrine has increased in scope. President Polk was the first to alter its fundamental character by holding, among other things, that the United States could not permit the peaceful transfer of American territory from one European nation to another, even if the inhabitants of the territory might desire the transfer to be made. By the process of interpretation, new items of prohibition have been added, until few of the matters which have disturbed the peace of mind of Americans lie beyond the scope of the historic doctrine.

From the promulgation of the Monroe Doctrine to the Civil War, the foreign policy of our government was concerned mainly with our "manifest destiny," which Theodore Roosevelt, before he became a public figure, pungently defined as our "destiny to swallow up the land of all adjoining nations who were too weak to withstand us."[2] Land hunger and love of adventure infected Americans with a keen desire to push their boundaries westward to the Pacific.

There were two obstacles in the way of westward expansion. Great Britain claimed ownership of the Oregon country, or at least part of it, while the vast region called Texas and the Californias was the property of Mexico. Both areas figured in

---

[2] Theodore Roosevelt, *Thomas N. Benton,* p. 40.

our diplomatic relations for many years, but Destiny (manifest or otherwise) decreed that Polk should be the president who would make the Pacific our western boundary. Texas declared its independence of Mexico in 1836 and sought admission into our Union, but as Mexico still asserted her claim to Texas, the proposal of the Lone Star republic was rejected.

In 1844 the Democratic party nominated Mr. Polk on a platform which demanded the "re-annexation of Texas" and the "re-occupation of Oregon." Nominated as a "dark horse," Polk proved to be a capable executive and an ardent expansionist. Before he entered the White House, however, President Tyler stole part of Polk's "thunder" by urging Congress to annex Texas by joint resolution. This was done, and Tyler signed the resolution three days before Polk's inauguration. Polk ordered General Taylor into Texas to protect it from a threatened invasion from Mexico, and within a few months a Mexican army crossed the Rio Grande and fired upon a detachment of Taylor's troops. Polk notified Congress that American blood had been shed upon American soil. He asked that body to recognize the war as a fact and to supply him with the means to prosecute it. As a result of this war, New Mexico and Upper California were added to the United States, partly by purchase and partly in settlement of debt claims against Mexico. A treaty with Great Britain settled the Oregon question by dividing the territory in dispute at the Forty-ninth Parallel. The task of "manifest destiny" had now been completed; the Pacific had been reached. If Americans coveted their neighbors' territories at a later date, it was for other reasons than land hunger.

During the decade and a half which preceded the Civil War, Americans were concerned mainly with the sectional controversy which Senator Seward christened the "irrepressible conflict," but two treaties were signed which were destined to play an important rôle in our foreign relations. The first was concluded in 1846, with New Granada, later called Colombia. It gave the United States the right of transit across the Isthmus of Panama; but, of more importance for later use, each of the parties guaranteed the neutrality of New Granada. The other was the Clayton-Bulwer treaty, signed in 1850.

Some time before this, Great Britain, by protectorates and other means, had acquired possession of the termini of a possible future canal. By the Clayton-Bulwer treaty it recognized the United States as an equal partner in the construction and control of such a canal. Many Americans thought this treaty to be a diplomatic victory; others regarded it as an infraction of the Monroe Doctrine and wished to have it abrogated, but England turned a deaf ear to all such overtures. We had to wait a half-century for "Downing Street" to change its mind.

The Civil War brought the usual crop of diplomatic controversies, such as that with Great Britain over the Confederate rams, and that with France concerning interference in Mexico; but these were the application of established practices rather than the formulation of new policies.

An opportunity was offered our government in this period to join with the leading European countries in an effort to protect neutral commerce in time of war. These European states had signed the Declaration of Paris in 1856, and invited the United States to sign the declaration. Its provisions exempted from capture both neutral goods on enemy ships and enemy goods on neutral ships except, of course, contraband of war. Another provision abolished privateering. The United States refused to sign the declaration unless all private property (except contraband), even enemy goods on enemy ships, should be exempt from capture. When this provision was rejected by the European signatories, our country declined to sign the original document. The Lincoln administration was willing to accept the unmodified declaration, in order to outlaw Confederate privateers; but for this very reason, the European countries were no longer willing to admit the United States as a party to the agreement of 1856. Once more we had maintained our policy of isolation.

The Civil War was followed by rapid internal development, especially in large industrial enterprises. At first, this affected mainly our national legislative program; but later it influenced our foreign policy as well.

Development of industries meant the creation of large corporations, better transportation, and new financial devices; but, more important for our present purpose, American manufacturers demanded a high protective tariff to minimize or exclude foreign competition. In time, however, our markets became saturated with American goods, and the producers desired an outlet for the surplus. South America and the Orient seemed to be the most promising fields for commercial penetration, and soon our foreign policy was influenced perceptibly by our desire to extend our commerce.

The Republican party had controlled the government since

the Civil War, and the first of its statesmen to see that high protective tariffs might at times be injurious to industry by limiting exports was James G. Blaine. As secretary of state in Garfield's cabinet, he sought to arrange reciprocity treaties with South American countries. But his tenure of office was cut short by Garfield's assassination and, besides, few of his party were interested in any scheme which would alter the policy of high protection.

Extension of our trade with the Orient, however, seemed possible without modifying the established protective policy; but successful competition with foreign nations in that area seemed to necessitate supply stations and naval bases along the way. In Harrison's administration, Hawaii was annexed, but his successor, Cleveland, withdrew the treaty from the Senate before it had been ratified. When the Republicans returned to power under McKinley, both the Orient and Latin America played important rôles in our foreign policy.

For some time Spain's administration in Cuba had caused irritation in the United States, but there was no actual interference in Cuban affairs. Urged on by Americans whose property interests were jeopardized in the island, President McKinley first protested against the Spanish policy in Cuba, and finally asked Congress to declare war against Spain. Commodore Dewey had already been ordered to Philippine waters, and when war had been declared he destroyed the Spanish fleet at Manila. Ere long, our government decided that Dewey's victory had obligated the United States to retain and to govern the islands. Of course, Spain was compelled to agree to the cession in the treaty which followed the war. We now had our stepping stones to the Asiatic coast, for Hawaii had been annexed after the Republicans returned to power. The process was completed by our assertion of the "Open Door" policy; that is, we demanded, successfully, that all doors must be left open to American commerce. In this same period South and Central America reëntered our foreign relations, but this time not in the form of reciprocal tariff treaties.

We have noted that the United States had endeavored repeatedly to induce Great Britain to abrogate the Clayton-Bulwer treaty, which had given the two nations equal control over a future isthmian canal. Down to the period of the Boer War, Great Britain had steadfastly refused to yield; but the Kaiser's famous telegram to President Kruger after the capture of the Jameson raiders, and other indications of German hostility, led John Bull to look about for friends. A European entente was, of course, of vital importance, but it would do no harm to gain the good will of the United States, should Europe become involved in war.

The trip of the battleship *Oregon,* round South America to join our fleet in Cuban waters, in our war with Spain, once more emphasized the necessity of shortening the distance between our coasts by the construction of an isthmian canal, and our government believed that it should be an American canal. So far, the Clayton-Bulwer treaty had stood in our way. This obstruction was removed more easily than had been expected, for John Bull was now in an amiable mood and eager to please his American cousin. The Hay-Pauncefote treaty of 1900 was negotiated without difficulty. By it Great Britain withdrew from the scene, and the United States was free to construct and own a canal as soon as it had made arrangements with the country through which the canal might pass. When the American Senate complained because we had not been given the right to fortify the canal, England conceded that point, also, in a treaty signed in 1901.

Although a canal through Nicaragua had strong advocates, the matter of route was settled by the signing of the Hay-Herran treaty with Colombia in January, 1903, which authorized the construction of a canal through the Isthmus of Panama. The refusal of the Colombian Senate to ratify this treaty unless certain provisions were altered, delayed but did not block the canal project. In characteristic fashion, President Roosevelt defined as blackmail the refusal of the Colombian Senate to ratify the treaty. In doing so, he seems to have forgotten his own defense of the United States Senate, only two years earlier, for declining to ratify the Hay-Pauncefote treaty unless our right to fortify the canal were conceded by England. On that occasion he wrote: " ... no treaty is a treaty until the Senate has confirmed it. .... No question of good faith or bad faith in any way enters into confirming or rejecting a treaty. The question is purely one as to the wisdom or unwisdom of the action sought."[3] This is the usual interpretation of the rights of any senate. Very conveniently, revolutionists in Panama declared their independence and thereby severed their connection with Colombia. Whether or not President Roosevelt aided this revolt by offering protection

[3] Roosevelt to Arthur Lee, March 18, 1901. In the Harding-Coolidge administration, Colombia was paid twenty-five million dollars "conscience money" because of Roosevelt's high-handed treatment of that country.

to the insurgents is a question which has been much debated; later, he said on the University's Berkeley campus, "I took the canal." Even if he did not participate in instigating the revolt, he was prompt in aiding the new Republic of Panama as soon as its independence had been declared. The first desideratum was to prevent interference by Colombia, and Professor John Bassett Moore had already indicated to the President how this might be done. Being a student of international relations, Moore remembered that in 1846 New Granada (i.e., Colombia) and the United States had signed a treaty in which each party had guaranteed the neutrality of the isthmus. This treaty, said Moore (and his pupil, the President), obligated the United States to prevent Colombia from repressing the insurrection in Panama. With equal promptness, Secretary Hay signed a treaty with Panama in which the new republic granted the concessions which the Colombian Senate had temporarily blocked.

The inauguration of President Wilson, in 1913, brought several changes in our foreign policy, although they did not prove to be permanent. He declined to use military force to protect property interests in Mexico merely because these interests were American and regardless of their merits. He declined to recognize a Mexican President who had obtained his office by violence, and he sought the aid of South American countries in solving the Mexican riddle. But the World War wrought the most spectacular change in our traditional foreign policy.

When the war began in 1914, President Wilson adhered to the isolation policy of Washington and Jefferson. He issued a neutrality proclamation and urged Americans to be neutral in thought as well as in deed. As the war progressed, we suffered the usual fate of neutrals; our commercial rights were frequently ignored by both belligerents, and the lives of our citizens were lost on the high seas. Confronted with these conditions, Mr. Wilson was willing to depart from the policy of isolation to the degree of offering mediation which might bring the war to an end; but when his offers were declined, he undertook the more difficult task of formulating a plan which, he hoped, would remove the causes of wars and prevent their recurrence in the future. When completed, his plan for eliminating international discords resembled, in many respects, Abraham Lincoln's policy for restoring harmony within the United States, during and following the Civil War. Both sought to eliminate blame, hate, and vengeance, and to make a peace based on abstract justice, with no attempt to determine which party to the conflict had been the original offender.

Naturally, Mr. Lincoln believed that the national government possessed the undoubted right, and was in duty bound, to preserve the Union and enforce its laws; but he never hated the Southern people for holding other views, nor did he wish to punish them for errors in judgment. After nearly four years of warfare, he said in his second inaugural address: "It may seem strange that any men should dare to ask a just God's assistance in wringing their bread from the sweat of other men's faces; but let us judge not, that we be not judged." The essence of his reconstruction policy may be found in another part of the same document, and it is this: "With malice toward none; with charity for all; with firmness in the right, as God gives us to see the right, let us strive on to finish the work we are in; to bind up the nation's wounds. . . . " Yes, his purpose was to bind up the wounds, not to rub salt into them or to wreak vengeance upon those who had resisted his authority. He recognized his late opponents as full-fledged American citizens, on terms of equality with citizens in other states, including the right to participate in governmental affairs—national, state, and local.[4] His death ended a policy based on good will and justice, and Congress substituted one based on vengeance, which engendered more sectional bitterness than had the war which preceded it.

Let us now turn to President Wilson's plan for ending the war and *reconstructing* the world. It may be found in his address to the United States Senate, delivered on January 2, 1917, before we had entered the war. The phrase most frequently quoted from it is "peace without victory." Detached from its context (which is customary), this seems to be a fantastic and preposterous proposal. As he gave and explained it, however, it is possible to consider it the greatest utterance of his life, for its aim was to remove the causes of war. From this address, I quote his own words:

"It is inconceivable that the people of the United States should play no part in that great enterprise [peace settlement]. . . ." Americans should "add their authority and their power to the authority and force of other nations to guarantee peace and justice throughout the world. Such a settlement cannot now be long postponed. It is right that before it comes

---

[4] Certain leaders were debarred temporarily from holding offices.

this Government should frankly formulate the conditions
upon which it would feel justified in asking our people to
approve its formal and solemn adherence to a League for
Peace. ... The treaties and agreements which bring it [the
war] to an end must embody terms which will create a peace
that is worth guaranteeing and preserving, a peace that will
win the approval of mankind, not merely a peace that will
serve the several interests and immediate aims of the nations
engaged ... it must be a peace without victory," because "victory would mean peace forced upon the loser, a victor's terms
imposed upon the vanquished. It would be accepted in humiliation, under duress, at an intolerable sacrifice, and would
leave a sting, a resentment, a bitter memory upon which
terms of peace would rest, not permanently, but only as upon
quicksand. Only a peace the very principle of which is equality and common participation in a common benefit. The right
state of mind, the right feeling between nations, is as necessary for a lasting peace as is the just settlement of vexed questions of territory or of racial and national allegiance.

"The equality of nations upon which peace must be founded
if it is to last must be an equality of rights. ... Equality of
territory or of resources there of course cannot be; nor any
other sort of equality not gained in the ordinary peaceful and
legitimate development of the peoples themselves. But no one
asks or expects anything more than an equality of rights.
Mankind is looking now for freedom of life, not for equi-
poises of power."

Like Lincoln, Wilson in formulating his reconstruction or
peace policy would make no attempt to fix the blame for

beginning the war. He would put aside hate and vengeance and arrange a settlement on the basis of abstract justice. The League of Nations was simply the executive authority to compel any recalcitrant member to respect the terms of settlement.

Again like Lincoln, he was unable to procure the adoption of his plan of peace based on justice. His colleagues at the peace council modified his terms of settlement, and his own country rejected his League of Nations.

Since omniscience is withheld from all, no one can say that the Wilsonian type of settlement would have been an absolute insurance against war. But we can say that the policy of vengeance and spoliation adopted at Versailles not only invited war but virtually guaranteed it, as soon as the vanquished or other dissatisfied members had mustered enough strength to repudiate the terms there imposed. The world was denied the opportunity to test a Wilsonian peace; it is now reaping the fruits of a peace *with* victory.

Since Wilson's administration, the United States has reverted to the policy of isolation. Having aided in defeating the League, President Harding suggested an "Association of Nations," but this anaemic substitute was quietly discarded. As its contribution to world peace, the Coolidge administration sponsored the Briand-Kellogg Peace Pact, the principal articles of which are:

Article I

The High Contracting Parties solemnly declare in the names of their respective peoples that they condemn recourse to war for the solution of international controversies, and renounce it as an instrument of national policy in their relations with one another.

Article II

The High Contracting Parties agree that the settlement or solution of all disputes or conflicts of whatever nature or of whatever origin they may be, which may arise among them, shall never be sought except by pacific means.

When more than thirty nations had approved this pact, it was proclaimed by President Hoover on July 24, 1929. Of course, such a condemnation of war is praiseworthy, but it resembles very much the annual New Year's resolutions of individuals. It is primarily a self-denying ordinance and does not include the mechanism or the power to make itself effective.

Even Mr. Wilson's own party seems content to limit its foreign policy to its own national affairs. We may ask, but cannot answer, this very important question: Can *national* and *international* welfare be totally separated? Should the present turmoil result in another world cataclysm, is it not possible that we may look with a more charitable eye on Wilson's *visionary* peace proposals, and deem them to have been more *practicable* than the settlement which he was forced to accept?

PAN AMERICA

HERBERT I. PRIESTLEY
PROFESSOR OF MEXICAN HISTORY
IN THE UNIVERSITY OF CALIFORNIA

Lecture delivered September 30, 1936

PAN AMERICA

A BOOK-REVIEWER recently used a descriptive phrase in which he said that a "sense of relationship between discrete events [is] the hall-mark of intelligence." Any effort to appraise this Western World or interpret our America as a part of man's social heritage with a modicum of appreciation of realities, must begin at its beginning, recalling what the world was like, in part, at the moment when the Red Man in the presence of Columbus gasped with a portentous apprehension, "Ah, at last we are discovered!" Next, we must be mindful of the courses of historic growth which have set us of the Occident into a world apart, yet bound us to our origins with unbreakable bonds, made us at once European and American, given us a detached Occidental point of view concerning the affairs of mankind, but made us also incapable of detaching ourselves and our fate from the common course of world affairs in which we are at one and the same time part cause and part effect.

A first approach to this appraisal may well take into account the relative position of America in the world of yesterday and of today, with some hope of estimating the direction of historic trends and envisaging the problems of tomorrow in their light. The distribution of Europeans about the world during four and a half centuries has had an effect, in what is usually called Europeanization, out of proportion to its numerical and political coefficients. For hundreds of years before Columbus, the expansive force of man had originated in Asia. To conjure the menace of the East, the Iberians, aided by mariners of Italy, turned to a new conception, that of the earth's roundness; they doubled the size of the world, brought into being new continents of thought and experience, recreated their own destinies. The Europeans have multiplied sixfold in the last three hundred years; their growth in numbers and their spread over the earth has been the outstanding fact in modern world history. During the historical process of his flight overseas, the relative potentiality of the European in the face of the non-European has risen, so that today his directive force upon the course of events and the influence of his culture is infinitely greater than when the tiny caravels of Columbus swung their prows into the west. Take, first of all, the significance of the changes in the numerical distribution of mankind on the several continents, changes caused in part by the discovery and growth of America.

When the world was still relatively young, say four hundred years ago, the population of Europe, as estimated recently by Huxley, was less than 100,000,000. In 1929 there were 642,000,000 Europeans, some 478,000,000 living in Europe. Outside of Europe were 164,000,000, of whom 13,000,000 were in Asia; the remainder, 151,000,000, lived overseas. Of the present population of the globe, 2,057,000,000, Asia comprises 1,121,000,000, or 54.5 per cent; Africa, which has added only 45,000,000 in three hundred years, has only 7 per cent of the total; the Western Hemisphere has 13 per cent, and Europe 25 per cent, of the inhabitants of the world. It cannot be said that overseas expansion did very much to reduce European population pressure. Indeed, through its influence upon the Industrial Revolution throughout its course, our hemisphere shares generously in responsibility for population growth in Europe.

At the present moment the increase of world population approaches stabilization. Future increase will be largely dependent upon fecundity of Asiatics and southern Europeans; for in northern Europe and America the population increase has reached a state of equipoise; even in Italy, Germany, and Japan, a balance is near, however strident their demands for growing-space. Oceania has not much more room. Africa is, so far, inhabitable by not many more Europeans. In the present state of political-mindedness of the peoples who yearn for colonies, significant pressure based upon economic needs and political aspirations will be brought to bear upon the less densely populated regions useful for habitation. Before millions now living shall pass away, the thinly populated regions of Africa and the Americas may feel the strain of demands upon their territorial capacity from millions more of Southern Europeans and Asiatics. Such a clash of interests must of course be modified by yet undeveloped changes in birth rates, accidents of nature, or the holocaust of general war.

The bearing of these population figures upon Pan American problems will emerge in a moment; just here it is pertinent to add, at risk of belaboring the obvious, that the Europeans have succeeded in planting political societies only in America, Australia and New Zealand, and South Africa. In North Africa the utmost hope of the French conqueror is that he may some day achieve the formation of a Berber-Latin empire. Quite as possibly, on the other hand, the Latin peoples of Europe may come to be ruled by Berber praetorian guards aligned with successful factions. In South Africa a composite society of two million Englishmen, Dutchmen, and French Huguenots lives with its back to a moving wall of six million non-Europeans, mostly black men, pressing down from the Soudan with ever increasing threat to white domination. In New Zealand 5 per cent of the population boasts a strain of native Maori blood; the "white Australia" policy confronts a possible invasion from the Malaysian swarms immediately to the north, driven southward by Mongoloid pressure. Even in the Americas the European stock has found the presence of the Indian a conditioning factor in its spread. Unmixed European stock in South America comprises only about thirty millions in the eighty millions of total population. In Mexico, the European is being gradually driven out as the natives develop political ambition and raise against the imperialism of foreigners a protective barrier of nationalistic legislation; and in internal affairs the Indian or the halfbreed (now growing rapidly in numbers) is coming to turbulent possession of the means of production and distribution, and seeking, with an eye turned toward recovery of the ascendency of the native culture, the evolution of his stock in the borrowed traditions and language of the erstwhile conqueror. In the Caribbean area, as a result of colonial slave-gang production of sugar and tobacco, a negroid population has been substituted for aborigines and conquerors alike. Into the United States the negroid population spread in the retinue of King Cotton; the fecundity of the black race and the process of miscegenation hold the prospect of the gradual tingeing of our population with various shades of black, so that students

of populations predict that one day we shall become one more
negroid republic. In South America, once sparsely settled regions have been taken over by scarcely assimilated, integral
colonies of millions of Italians and Spaniards, a million Germans, and more than two hundred thousand Japanese. At
any moment some diplomatic incident may bring these nonpolitical colonies into international significance of grave concern to the United States. Lust for expansion may yet call for
new enunciation of an American defense policy. In several
South American countries immigration control comparable
to our own of 1926 is in operation. In South Africa, Australia,
and North America north of Mexico, there has been a determination to maintain European stocks pure from so-called
lower-culture admixtures; in all those regions the threat to
purity of European stock is actual or potential. In Asia and
the Near East the white race, so long dominant in economic
relations and political influence, is on the way out; instance
Japan, China, India, Egypt, Syria. In Siberia and Eastern
Asia, the population trend is dependent upon the interplay
of Europe and Asia in a problem cognate with but separated
from our own. Perhaps the world is entering a period in
which international politics will be dominated less and less
by European interests, more and more by what were once
called "lesser breeds without the law."

Be that as it may, it is patent that the "expansion of Europe"
has been more widely successful in the economic and cultural
than in the political field; that of the five great nations which
concerned themselves with political domination over the
extra-European world, the Iberian nations and the British

were the only ones that transplanted societies as monuments to their overseas activities. The Spaniard and the Englishman, with some help from the French, as in Quebec and Haiti, gave America to Europe and Europe to America. On this continent the destinies of their descendants mingle in twenty-one republics and one independent Dominion.

So much then for the place of Pan America, judged by numerical ratios, possible population movements, and transplanted nations, in the world of yesterday and today. But what are the political and international implications of this phenomenal development? Since the Wars of Independence, the Americas have been dominated by two ideals, one the maintenance of their separation from Europe, the other the search for a formula for continental unity. The term "Pan America" was an idealization rather than a reality at the moment of South American liberation; it was based upon distrust of the European states from which the Spanish and English societies of America had been freed, upon an equally shared desire to keep the Western Hemisphere free from further incursions of colonizing states, and upon the assumption that we had all been only precariously freed from the evils of monarchism and exploitation, and were bound together by common ideals of democracy and liberalism.

At the time this country of ours gained its independence, the population of England was nine millions, and that of North America entire was about five millions, some three millions being in the thirteen colonies. It was not superior strength, nor success in a final test of military power, but the unhappy condition of England in the face of its European opponents, which gave the decision at arms to the American revolutionaries. For many years weight was given to the apprehension of Franklin lest some attempt at reconquest might develop. When the states of Europe which had been threatened by the ascendency of Napoleon had conjured that menace, they turned to undoing the damage to the monarchical and the mercantilist system wrought by the propaganda for democracy which had helped into existence the United States, revolutionized France, and presaged the revolt of the colonies of Spain after the example of the Anglo-American neighbor. To the apparent determination of the Holy Alliance to restore the departing colonies of Spain to the system of European monarchy, but more especially to the chaotic condition in which American territory had been left when the United States entered the Family of Nations, was the noncolonization clause of the Monroe Doctrine addressed. In the words of John Bassett Moore:

... to the founders of the American Republic the question of territorial expansion did not present itself as a matter of speculation, or even of choice. There was not a single European Power having possessions in America that did not lay claim to more territory than it had effectively occupied, nor was there a single one whose claims were not contested by some other Power; and these contests were interwoven with the monopolistic struggle then in progress for colonial commerce and navigation. The Spaniards and the Portuguese, the English and the French, the Swedes and the Dutch, contended with one another in Europe, as well as in America for empire on the American continents. Their colonists knew no rule of life but that of conflict; and they regarded the extension of their boundaries as a measure of self-defense rather than of aggression.

At the moment of independence the Swedes and the Dutch had been eliminated, but the others remained, with problems of boundaries and commerce, with only a short time to pass before Russia was to be added as one more potential threat to our independence and expansion.

The noncolonization declaration was an effort to bring to an end the centuries of strife that had characterized the partitioning of the New World; uttered as an idea basic to our own security, by the same token it was a safeguard to the nascent Spanish American states, recognizing their welfare as part of our own, and as such has been frequently lauded by their statesmen. But it is equally true that the failure to include any inhibition against our own acquisition of Spanish territory (a lack which prevented our joining Great Britain in a self-denying clause concerning conquests) is one of the leading causes of the dissatisfaction with which our ideal of Pan America has been viewed among our Latin neighbors. The fact that the United States has, since independence, acquired territory almost five times as large as the original thirteen colonies, most of it at the expense of Spanish American neighbors, is basic in the doctrines of hostility to us which have long been preached in the countries south of the Río Grande. Even in the words of Henry Adams, than whom there has probably never been a historian with greater sense of propriety:

In the end, far more than half the territory of the United States was the spoil of the Spanish Empire, rarely acquired with perfect propriety. To sum up the story in a single word, Spain had immense influence over the United States; but it was the influence of the whale over its captors,—the charm of a huge, helpless, and profitable victim.

Of these dissatisfactions just mentioned, it may be said in passing that in large part they are the fruit not only of our aggressions, but also of conscious propaganda, for business advantage, by individuals and groups unofficially representing European countries. Some of these capitalize on our business mistakes, and the bad manners sometimes shown by our travelers; magazines and newspapers have labored our lack of intellectual community. Columnists use us as a theatrical property to stir up the bogey of distrust. Politicians threaten opponents with defeat if they show us friendship or accept our aid. Care is taken in Europe to conserve South American relations; even such a world-wise sheet as the *Manchester Guardian* desires, amid tariff preferentials, no mistake regarding Argentina, "which we have always considered," remarks the editor, "an economic province of the British Empire."

The Monroe Doctrine was an effort to establish the idea of a reciprocal respect for the separation of the new hemisphere from the old without commitments which would limit the prospective growth of the United States. Comparable to this Doctrine, and following it by barely more than a year, was the letter penned on December 7, 1824, by Simón Bolívar, President of Peru for the moment, suggesting a conference of the independent American states at Panama. Bolívar's conception was not marked by ungratified hankering for territorial expansion, but it sought a secure position for rebellious states not yet fully independent. The United States was omitted from the invitation, perhaps because of our retention of African slavery, perhaps because we were not companions of their revolt, perhaps because we were logical heirs of the old antipathy of England for Spain. Later, at the suggestion of Mexico and Colombia (somewhat ironically, in view of our attitude toward their espousal of Cuban independence and our later conquests from Mexico, and our troubles with Colombia in the Canal episode) the United States was included in the invitation, and accepted it under the urge of Henry Clay, early champion of Spanish American democracy. No less genuine in his espousal of the idea was President John Quincy Adams, who declared that the convocation would "form a new epoch in human affairs," provided it be kept free from legislative capacity and confined to diplomatic recommendations. Bickerings over internal politics kept us from rising to the full measure of this early opportunity for continental leadership.

Bolívar's aim was essentially to draw together the weak Latin states fighting to be free from mother Spain, and to draw the United States to their support, an aim as much self-interested as the Monroe Doctrine. But it was a much more precarious proposal, since it depended on the joint action of several states, while Monroe's was unilateral. Our failure in 1826 was only less destructive to the plan of union than our later acquisition of Texas and of the present Southwest. Equally disturbing to the plan for continental coöperation were the results of the Conference among the Spanish states— for only four of them attended, and of ten proposals in as many treaties, only one was ratified and that by a single state.

Heartbroken Bolívar, viewing the nonfulfillment of his dreams, breathed his disillusionment in the tragic words, "I have ploughed in the sea."

Implicit in his union was the idea of the political and diplomatic isolation of the Americas from Europe, the same doctrine of the "two spheres" evolved by Thomas Jefferson and his forerunners in the days of the formation of the North American republic. Explicit and frequent were the complaints because we refused to take up arms for the independence of the struggling states.

Invitations were repeatedly issued by Mexico for further conferences in 1831, 1838, 1839, and 1840, to effect "a union and close alliance for the purpose of defense against foreign invasion, the acceptance of free mediation in the settlement of all disputes ... between the sister republics, and the framing and promulgation of a code of public law regulating their mutual relations." Meetings could not be held because of revolutions; the Texan episode was background to most of the efforts of Mexico, by alliances to check our territorial sweep.

Again in 1847, five South American states assembled at Lima to take measures to insure the "independence, sovereignty, dignity, and territorial integrity of the republics present." At that moment the United States, though invited, was at war with Mexico. No practical results were achieved.

In 1856, Chile brought together three South American states which signed, but did not ratify, a continental treaty. The United States was not invited. Fear of William Walker and other filibusters constituted one reason for the call of this congress. In actuality Walker was eliminated by France and

Great Britain rather than by the United States, though our government did withdraw the mistaken recognition which the Marysville and San Francisco adventurer had obtained from Secretary Marcy. Again, in 1864, a convention of certain Spanish American nations at Lima undertook to abolish war by arbitration. The Republic of Colombia, in accepting, requested that the United States be omitted because its policy was adverse to alliance and because its preponderance in deliberations would embarrass the conference. This was the last of the American conferences on Latin initiative hostile to the United States but laboring toward realization of a continental ideal.

In 1870, when war was being waged by Spain against the western American countries, the United States, as a neutral, convoked the nations concerned in a conference at Washington, and those Powers in 1871 suspended the war indefinitely, notice of resumption of hostilities to be issued through the United States. Again, in the "Nitrate War" by Chile against Peru and Bolivia in 1877–83, an arbitration treaty was signed proposing to ask the President of the United States to mediate. These more friendly reactions of the southern republics occurred because of Lincoln's opposition to the French invasion of Mexico. The end of the war in the Pacific came in a convention which included the proposal: "The settlement by arbitration of each and every international controversy shall become a principle of American public law."

In November, 1881, began the important move by Secretary Blaine to gather all the American republics in Washington for a conference which was deferred by political accidents till 1889; it was proposed to establish a conscious union and plan for arbitration of all American international disputes; in addition, numerous improvements in business relations were contemplated. None of the treaties negotiated at the time was ratified, but Blaine's conspicuous success was the formation of the Bureau of American Republics. Organized for mutual advantages in culture and commerce, the Bureau was dominated, during the earlier years, by the latter purpose. Recent efforts, however, have tended to develop the real community of interests, more frequently cultural. When after fifty years of struggle the Clayton-Bulwer treaty was abrogated by express declaration of the Hay-Pauncefote treaty, our naval supremacy in the Caribbean introduced to our country an added responsibility for defense. The Spanish American War had opened a new chapter in the life of the continent.

In 1901 and 1902, the second international American conference at Mexico, generally attended, arranged that all the American states, now including republican Brazil, should join the Hague Convention of 1899 for the pacific settlement of disputes. It drafted a treaty for compulsory arbitration of pecuniary claims, which was signed by seventeen states including ourselves. Our liberation of Cuba, followed by its forced acceptance of the Platt Amendment, together with the assumption about this time of police duty over Latin American debtor nations by Theodore Roosevelt—the socalled "Roosevelt Corollary" of the Monroe Doctrine—loaded us with an onerous burden, later removed to a degree by Philander P. Knox in his refunding of Latin American debts through New York investment houses. The police function, long a topic of bitter Latin jeremiads, was repudiated in 1923 by Reuben Clark in his historical survey of the Monroe Doctrine.

The third conference at Buenos Aires, in 1910, drafted a number of treaties concerning commercial affairs, and enlarged the Bureau of American Republics and changed its name to Pan American Union. In the year 1912 came the adoption of the Lodge Resolution by our Senate, expanding the defensive quality of the Doctrine to prospective intrusions by Asiatic Powers.

The fifth conference, scheduled for 1914 but postponed until 1923 because of the Great War, reached agreements only general, but one of them, the Gondra treaty, provided for a fact-finding commission to investigate international disputes. The treaty followed the lines of the Bryan conciliation treaties of 1916 and the treaty of February, 1923, between the United States and the republics of Central America. It was noteworthy as an exclusively American agreement providing that American disputes should be settled by American means. This meeting, although marred by asperities, did initiate reforms in the structure of the Pan American Union and did begin formal international intellectual coöperation. It failed to effect an international disarmament agreement, or to accept the proposal of Uruguay to establish an American League of Nations. The outstanding declaration by our representative, Mr. Fletcher, that the Monroe Doctrine is a unilateral enunciation of policy, was badly received. Secretary Hughes's later definition of the Doctrine as opposed to en-

croachment by us, in any guise, on the political independence of Spanish American states, and against the acquisition
or control of territory in America by any non-American
power, missed the point of the Latin American objections,
namely, the dread of far-reaching effects of economic penetration by the United States and our assumption of tutelary
control. Part of the hostility was owing to the imagined pos-
sibility that our naval mission to Brazil was a thinly veiled
mode of extending our national control. Our so-called traditional amity with that country has been of no advantage to
our relations with the Spanish-speaking countries. The belief
prevailed that the United States was concealing a purpose of
political domination and commercial absorption. The resistance to the United States has, however, been popular rather
than official. The insistence of Mexico that she refuse to
recognize the Doctrine is a hopeless assertion of attitude, in
view of that country's geographical location within the pe-
riphery of our Canal policy; it also reveals that country as
apparently forgetful of our help in the Maximilian episode,
while mindful of the conquests of 1846–48.

At the time of the Great War in Europe, the test of our
leadership came when, at the invitation of President Wilson
to all neutral governments to follow our declaration of war,
only eight Powers did so, although five others broke relations
with Germany. The only active coöperation against the Central Powers was by Brazil and Cuba. The notorious sympathy
of Mexico and Argentina for the Central Powers made it obvious that Pan Americanism was an aspiration rather than an
actuality at the moment of large-scale intervention in Europe.

Nevertheless, the ideal of a Pan American solidarity which shall include the United States has been at various times defended by South American notables like Agustín Edwards of Chile, Oliveira Lima of Brazil, Federico Pezet of Peru, and Rómulo S. Naon of Argentina. These gentlemen have opposed the Latin American League from time to time invoked by publicists and *littérateurs* whose pose and need of a thesis evokes a perennial Yankeephobia. Tancredo Pinochet, in his *Gulf of Misunderstanding,* and Manuel Ugarte, in the *Destiny of a Continent,* have echoed the dictum of Blanco-Fombona that "the Yankees are the enemies of our souls, characters and independence." Popular criticism of our recent activities in Cuba and Puerto Rico is sometimes as bitter as though no "good neighbor policy" had ever been declared. Most of our critics have tried to offset the influence of the United States by establishing cultural relations with Spain, Portugal, France, or Italy, their efforts not having gone without welcoming response. The idea of a Latin league meets with little success, however, because Latin American solidarity is farther from actual realization than Pan Americanism. The reorganization suggested for the Pan American Union in 1923 looked toward selection of representatives other than the ambassadors in the hope of making the Union independent of the United States. It also sought to have the directorship rotate among the nations. Inasmuch as decisions by the Union must be unanimous, most of these efforts awaited developments, but the idea was accepted that the chairman should be elective and not the United States' secretary of state by right. It was agreed that if a state has no diplomatic relations with us, it may appoint a representative to the Union—as, for example, Mexico, which from 1920 to 1923 had no ambassador in Washington, hence no place in the Conference. The choice of separate representatives has as yet received no confirmation. Changes in the structure of the Union are not likely to weaken the position of the United States as long as we lead in commercial activity, wealth, and naval force. But if a league should be organized excluding the United States, or if the Union should undertake to make political decisions by majority vote, our position would become difficult.

The sixth conference, held at Havana in January, 1928, found for the first time all the twenty-one republics represented. The moment was critical for our influence. For the first time our President (Coolidge) attended the convocation, and Secretary Hughes took an important part. They sought to sidetrack discussion of the topic of intervention, then to the fore because of the Nicaraguan muddle. Mexico opposed a number of its sister states which wanted to inject political discussion. Argentina was insistent that tariff difficulties be discussed, that country being a debtor state which finds difficulty concerning the admission of its raw products into the United States. The subject of intervention was three times intruded into the debates, against the wishes of many members, especially of those from the United States. As a solution, Doctor Maurtua, one of the jurists present, made the proposal that the Union should declare that "every nation has a right to exist, and to protect and conserve its existence, but this right neither implies the right nor justifies the act of preservation by the commission of unlawful acts against innocent and unoffending states. Every nation has the right to independence in the same sense that it has the right to the pursuit of happiness, and is free to develop without influence or control from other states, providing that in so doing it does not interfere with nor violate the rights of other states." Secretary Hughes's approval of this declaration as a new Magna Charta was opposed by all the Latin states except Cuba, Nicaragua, and Haiti, which were then under our strong arm. The earnest efforts of several administrations to bring our armed occupations of Caribbean countries to an end have partly restored confidence in our sincerity. The final conclusion of the labors of the Mexico-United States Mixed Claims Commissions, upon the "ability to pay" basis, our acceptance of Mexican nationalistic legislation, our refusal to intervene in the religious controversy, and the fact that no compulsion has been exerted to adjust payment of many millions of defaulted Latin American bonds held in the United States, are evidences of changing times and of modification in the art of financial international relations.

Since 1919, opposition to the Monroe Doctrine centers on the tacit assumption, in the unhappy phrase of the League Covenant, whereby that body is not to interfere with "regional understandings." Being unilateral and interpreted and applied by executive action of the United States, the Doctrine is certainly anything but a regional understanding, and means to the Latin mind that we pretend to assert plain tutelage at discretion. Whenever the Doctrine has been complicated by debt collection, canal strategy, protection of life and property, "dollar diplomacy," and governmental efforts to stop revolution as a normal renovation of offices, it has been openly questioned, as by Salvador, and officially disapproved. The Havana conference did make progress by adopting resolutions governing right of asylum, duties of neutrals in civil strife, maritime neutrality treaties, diplomatic and consular agents, and status of foreigners, together with a number of commercial agreements. In spite of the intervention quarrel, the meeting was "second to none in formulation of actual measures to promote inter-American coöperation and solidarity."

The seventh conference, held at Montevideo in December, 1933, adopted ninety-five resolutions and six conventions, concerned with the organization of peace, principles of intervention, an inter-American nonaggression pact, neutrality, extradition, rights and duties of states, and economic and financial questions. Provision was made for multilateral economic treaties, on a most-favored-nation basis of reciprocity, over a wide area. In spite of the peace machinery set up at the Washington Conference on Arbitration and Conciliation in 1929, to handle disputes not amenable to diplomacy, the Chaco War and the Leticia dispute had demonstrated the notorious failure of the peace movement; the Chaco War was in full swing during the session of the Conference. The League of Nations was here interested in a purely American situation, with a representative at the Union meeting; its previous failure through arms embargo and threat of sanctions to effect a settlement threw the problem back upon the South American neighbors. An attempt was made to strengthen conciliation machinery by creating a permanent delegation for the purpose. Its nonpolitical character was considered its chief weakness. Mexico's move toward an American League of Nations by establishment of an Inter-American Court of Justice and an Inter-American Labor Office was without result.

The reason for inability to stop the Chaco War was that the disputants were not signatory to any one of the pacts covering the situation, or had not both ratified them. Even the Kellogg Pact proved toothless, as elsewhere. But it is not true that our Latin neighbors prefer war to pacific settlement. They were the first, after our Jay treaty of 1794, to promise arbitration; Colombia, Peru, and Chile entered such an agreement in 1822, and others soon followed. At Panama, in 1826, conciliation and mediation were agreed upon. The same ideals were sought in 1847 at Lima, in 1856 at Santiago, and in 1864 at Lima again, as has been said.

Many states have taken unilateral action toward the same end; Brazil in her 1891 and 1934 constitutions promised to use war only when arbitration should fail, and never to make war for conquest, whether in alliance or alone. Uruguay, Venezuela, and Santo Domingo have the same unilateral declarations.

Most of these states have applied mediation, conciliation, or arbitration in peaceful settlements of vexed boundary difficulties. While the Chaco dispute was on, a tribunal in Washington composed of a Chilean, a Costa Rican, and the United States Chief Justice settled the Guatemala-Honduras boundary, and it has been marked by monuments. Santo Domingo and Haiti at the same time settled their boundary quarrel by direct negotiations. The Latin states have settled peacefully more disputes than have led to war. War today is less likely in the Americas—the Western Hemisphere—than in any other part of the world; it is barely possible that this may be as much owing to a century of peace propaganda as to natural conditions. The other American states from 1928 on tried hard to get Bolivia and Paraguay to make peace. The peace protocol of June 12, 1935, was the result of coöperation between eight American republics—Argentina, Bolivia, Brazil, Chile, Paraguay, Peru, Uruguay, and the United States. The "Roerich Pact," signed at Washington on April 15, 1935, promised that twenty-one American republics would protect artistic and scientific institutions, whether in peace or war. "This brings renewed allegiance," said Franklin Roosevelt, "to those high principles of international coöperation which will be a great contribution to civilization by the Americas."

On October 10, 1933, there was signed at Rio an antiwar pact initiated by Dr. Saavedra Lamas of Argentina and now adhered to by all the American republics, which condemns wars of aggression and declares that controversies shall be settled by pacific means; it refuses recognition of territory acquired by force, and provides a procedure for conciliation.

From the Chaco dispute as a basis and from its protocol, Franklin Roosevelt, on June 30, 1936, began to move for a special Inter-American Conference to Preserve Peace, whether through the prompt general ratification of existing treaties, their amendment, or by a new common accord. "The conference will meet [in December], rich in a heritage of devotion to and actual application of the principles of conciliation and arbitration, constituting, by that very circumstance, a happy

augury for the success of its deliberations." It should prove
to be the greatest contribution of the American republics
to the conduct of international relations and to the solidarity
of the continent. One of its chief aims will be to prevent
American states from being drawn into European wars. It is
a noteworthy effort to provide for the neutrality of a whole
hemisphere when peace fails elsewhere.

Following the Chaco settlement treaty, too many others to
mention were celebrated among the A B C P group, which
laid foundations for preservation of the spirit of friendship.

The lavishly documented peace movement described has
not been the sole field of Pan American coöperation. We in
the United States should not forget that in current times
there has been a noticeable easing of the strain upon our Latin
American relations. This is not because we have given up
anything essential. The abrogation of the Platt Amendment
by treaty under the present administration accounts in part
for the easement. Even with Mexico, a country with which
there are problems that still require adjustment, there is a
calm contrasting happily with long years of misunderstanding. The spirit with which Argentina is coöperating in the
coming December Peace Conference shows a growing sentiment of continental responsibility. But it cannot be forgotten
that in Cuba, dedicated to sugar monoculture, a sugar tariff
is a means of effective tutelage. The notes of disharmony
coming from university students in Cuba, from Mexican rad-
icals, and from *littérateurs* whose stock in trade would vanish
were harmony restored, are like our one-time sport of twist-
ing the British lion's tail: they cannot vitiate the entire pro-

gram of the Conference or the growth of a continental sense. They are expressions of Latin individualism, echoes of a mistrust grounded not so much in politics as in realization of the disadvantage of the Latin nontechnical mind face to face with our technical ability and financial resources in an industrialized and mechanized age. They are essentially self-challenges to Latin American youth to rise more adequately to the demands of the new age and enlarge their capacities to compete successfully with a rapidly changing world. The same voices would be raised against any European society which might suggest an attitude of leadership. In a moment of menace, the hated "Doctrine" would be appealed to, and the idea of "fiat" prove more welcome than when voiced by Secretary Olney. It is no doubt true, as Professor Torres says, that the coming Peace Conference idea is accepted more readily as a proposal from the United States than from any of the other republics. It may even be hoped that the Peace Plan there to be developed may have some relevant suggestion useful to a threat-bedeviled Europe.

There are not to be omitted from further appraisal certain undeniable advantages which Pan America possesses over Europe and Asia and Africa. Governmentally organized in twenty-one republics, we all are, at least formally, adherents of republican ideals; our cultural neighborhood is helped by the fact that we speak only four European languages in the entire hemisphere. English is a practical *lingua franca*. We have an almost universal decimal currency, many monetary systems being the same as that of the United States. We have but two or three religions, none of them modernistic, to

which adhesion is given by large groups. We have wide ranges
of sympathy, as has been evidenced in the United States by a
generous appreciation and absorption of Spanish American
art. Reciprocity treaties between the United States and half
a dozen Latin American states offer opportunities for mutual
profit. The *Pan American Bulletin,* published in the three
most useful languages, contains a wealth of intellectual food,
and a healthful propaganda of information and understanding. Had such a publication been imitated in Europe successfully for the past half-century, it might have helped to
make that unhappy continent something other than a waste
of old shambles of 1918, with new graves yawning for millions more young men who may soon march forth to make
the world safe for Communism or Fascism, or to a war to end
war in mutual extermination. No iniquitous Treaty of Versailles ever hung over the self-respect of an American nation
on either continent.

Other factors tending to unify Pan America are worth
enumerating: By our Postal Union a letter goes from the
Canadian border to Patagonia for three cents—less than it
costs us to write to mother England; our airlines girdle the
hemisphere in a few short days; railways, steamboats, automobile roads, insure rapid and cheap communications. An
International High Commission, a Committee for Codifica-
tion of International Law, a Committee on International Intellectual Coöperation, and many other agencies scientific or
bibliographical, share the effort to keep the various parts in
touch, all emphasizing the policy of coöperation, based upon
the philosophy of the legal equality of states.

What, on the other hand, are unfulfilled possibilities? Some of the needs we might work toward are wider mutual diffusion of English, Spanish, and Portuguese for adequate understanding. In the United States there is need of more appreciation of the literary and scientific ability of South Americans through better organization of the book trade of those countries. It is of interest that a recent *Who's Who in Latin America* edited on the level of our own *Who's Who* includes twelve hundred names in categories the same as ours, omitting crooners. There is needed a readier acceptance of Latin American students in our colleges and universities. These higher institutions of learning can increase their usefulness without sacrifice of standards by offering more workable entrance facilities to competent Latin American students, who will return to their own countries having enriched our experience by their coming, themselves by new points of view gained, and their peoples by more adequate understanding of our technical evolution and our intellectual life.

But before and after and beyond details of adjustment, we want to bear in mind that, beneath all their different traits, due to ethnic origins and varied habitat in the Occident, the colonizers of America have a common tradition, under varying guises, of long struggle for the liberalization of the human mind and soul. The fight of the republican government of Spain to preserve respect for an accepted constitution, adequate opportunity for the worker, and majority rule established by lawful election, is one more echo of the heroic struggle by the communes of the sixteenth century against imperial Charles V. The rebel forces, representing ob-

scurantism, supremacy of privileged classes, absentee land-
lords, and the socially irresponsible, win a military decision,
but they merely delay the victory of democracy, the right of
the impoverished peasant to a civilized living. In the end the
movement toward liberalization and integration must win;
the opposite is social suicide. Spain's daughters among
American states, with all their dissimilarities and intermix-
tures of blood, carry the genes of an urge toward self-realiza-
tion and self-expression which are of the essence of freedom
and of human existence; a freedom not merely from foreign
invasion or alien penetration, or from the inferiority complex
arising from technological retardation and insufficiency of
economic experience and organization, but also a freedom
arising from the enduring sense of the value and sacredness
of the individual, which rose to a high plane in our own War
of Independence, found expression again in the French Revolution, gathered force under the inspiration of Andrew
Jackson, and had its exemplars in the Liberators of Spanish
America. Unhappily, those new-born nations were carried
away by the glamour of republican organization before they
could recuperate the virtues of their former representative
government through town procurators, the humble beginnings of which were snuffed out in New Spain by the same
Charles V who killed the development of municipal vitality
on the battlefield of Villalar. Since gaining their independence, those nations have been swarmed by foreign *conquista-
dores* who have monopolized their business and industry,
and left to their peoples the mere husks of political existence,
the desire to feed at the crib of public office, and to levy ex-

tortions upon the aliens, producers of wealth such as they have not been able to develop from their own nationals because of the accidents of birth, bent, and training. The economic situation explains why so often democracy is supplanted by dictatorship among Latin Americans. Over against these defects, accidental or intrinsic, as you will, they have in their souls the inherent capacity to survive disaster and apparent annihilation, their rich heritage of resistance through four hundred years of unceasing disaster, in the blood of their American Indian forebears.

With such heritage and such need, our fellow Americans challenge us to the conscious direction of our own social force into the channels indicated by our origins. It is a philosophy of defeatism which bewails the end of the liberal tradition and an inevitable yielding to class struggle. The dawn of the new age which followed the discovery of America was illumined by the liberal tradition, the aspirations of the people, whether Spanish or English.

If we have been exercising that "sense of the relationship between discrete events" which ought to be our hall-mark, we have found the problem of Pan America to be bound up in the world problem and not to be separated from it by political devices, though it is conditioned by environment. The search for life, liberty, and the pursuit of security is centuries old and continents wide; it owns to no differences of color, creed, national lines, or dividing seas. Formulas, isms, and systems do little to change the essential character of the struggle or to modify human motives. With reasonable honesty, reasonable intelligence, we may preserve intact the heritage

of the New World, if not in anticipation of "the judgment
of history," whatever that may mean, at least under obligation
to maintain for *our own day an optimum* of effective government, social equity, and economic well-being.

THE UNITED STATES AND EUROPE:
ISOLATION OR COÖPERATION?

———

ROBERT J. KERNER
PROFESSOR OF MODERN EUROPEAN HISTORY
IN THE UNIVERSITY OF CALIFORNIA

Lecture delivered October 7, 1936

THE UNITED STATES AND EUROPE: ISOLATION OR COÖPERATION?

M ARK TWAIN once said the first trip to Europe was always a mistake. One tried to do and to see too many things in too short a time and the result was very disappointing. In the World War the United States took its first trip to Europe with similar consequences: it was a mistake.

Please note that the emphasis in Mark Twain's remarks was on the word "first"; the implication is that it takes more than one trip to know and to understand Europe. Some Americans have had their first trip. A very few have had more than one. But the sad thing is that at present most of the Americans who have never had even a first trip to Europe are the experts on the subject. This is especially true of the distinguished and eloquent Senator from Idaho.

One meets also with this experience. An artist finally concludes a long conversation with the remark, "Well, one man's opinion is as good as another's." When the retort is, "Indeed! Do you mean that when it comes to art, one man's opinion is as good as another's?" the artist almost gets a stroke of apoplexy and bursts into rage with the remark, "No shoemaker is going to tell me what is art!" Now, one could substitute a hundred other such experts on Europe in the place of the artist and get exactly the same remark for his trouble.

Then there is the person who believes that anything that is against his prejudices or reveals his ignorance is anti-German, or anti-Italian, or anti-Bolshevik. To criticize the policy of a ruler is not only anti-Hitler or anti-Mussolini, but anti-

German or anti-Italian. By the same logic, if one criticizes the policy of the President of the United States, he is anti-American. If these views cannot be discarded by a university audience, it is idle for a scholar, whose profession and purpose is truth and objectivity, to say anything whatsoever, for it is only through observation, comparison, and criticism that the truth can be revealed.[1]

EUROPE IN THE PERSPECTIVE

In the evolution of present-day Europe—and for that matter, the rest of the world—we note, in the perspective, two dominant historical forces, nationalism and economic interdependency.[2] They originated in or were stimulated chiefly by the American, French, and Industrial Revolutions, and are now operating with all their power for good or evil. The first-named and older force, nationalism, has triumphed over all other forces and is today the most powerful. In its wake, the world is being decentralized politically. Mistakenly called Balkanization, the process really started in Western Europe in the Middle Ages and spread from there to the rest of the world. Ancient empires have been transformed or destroyed by it. The Spanish empire, the Austro-Hungarian empire,

---

[1] In a popular lecture limited to one hour it is not possible to discuss all problems or to enter into their many complicated details. The emphasis is on aspects connected with the title of the lecture series. A few references are given here for the benefit of students desiring to get an introduction to a small part of the mass of evidence upon which the speaker has drawn.

[2] This conception of the duality of the dominant historical forces, original with the speaker, was advanced by him in public addresses before and since the World War. It appeared in print for the first time in his "The Prospects of Peace in Europe" (*American Academy of Political and Social Science*, July, 1932).

and the Ottoman empire have crumbled before it. New nations have emerged from their ruins. The British empire has saved itself thus far by transforming itself into a Commonwealth of Nations—a sort of league of nations. The old Russian empire is now a federation (with subfederations) of nations under the title of the Union of Soviet Socialist Republics. Everywhere nationalism or its seeming contradiction, national imperialism, is on the increase. It goes without saying that it is both a good and an evil and that man must learn how to control it.

The other historical force, economic interdependency, though younger in years than nationalism, is operating likewise with increasing force and virulency. The recent scamper to cover by nearly all nations behind extreme policies of economic nationalism or isolation only proves it the more conclusively. But it also proves that down to this point in history nationalism is stronger than economic interdependency. Born of the Industrial Revolution, which is transforming not only industry and commerce, but agriculture as well, this historical force is working in direct opposition to the politically disintegrating effects of nationalism. It is making the world economically interdependent, whether we will it or no. It is welding the world into a vast economic unit, into a world economy with catastrophic consequences to those who oppose it. Such is probably in large part the explanation of the World Depression. That it is both a good and an evil, and that man must learn to control it, likewise goes without saying.

By drawing attention to the clash of these forces, we may

be able to explain objectively the Prewar Era from 1870, the World War and its Peace Settlements, and the Postwar Period. In fact, the World War and the World Depression were the first great world-wide demonstrations of the clash of these opposing historical forces. In proportion as we have sought to explain the recent history of Europe in terms of individuals, single nations, special classes, or local color, we have failed to understand what is going on. Each individual, each nation, or each class has been caught in the whirl of these historic forces far more powerful than any individual, nation, or class. Each is trying to explain its policy and its actions without reference to the situation as a whole and yet each has its particular and often peculiar part to play in the tragedy of our times. The catastrophes of the World War and the World Depression significantly prove that they are not local phenomena and that man has not been able to grapple with world-wide forces with such organization as he has been able to improvise. The personal, national, or class devil has been sought and harried about hither and yon when effort might better have been directed toward the adjustment, balance, and control of the forces of nationalism and economic interdependency. Individuals, nations, and classes are what they are because of the clash of these forces.

THE PREWAR PERIOD

The Prewar Period may be said to begin approximately with the Franco-Prussian War in 1870. This war, it will be remembered, began with the creation of the first German Reich by the proclamation and the brandishing of swords in France's

Holy of Holies, the Hall of Mirrors in Versailles, by the erection of the Bismarck statue in Berlin of cannon cast from the gold of the French indemnity, by the creation of the war chest of gold at Spandau, and the building of multiple lines of tracks for fast railroads to the French frontier from the same source. The most-favored-nation privilege acquired by Germany in the markets of France, as well as the loss of the remnant of the Saar coal field, by the Treaty of Frankfort, became a great obstacle to economic development and the growth of industry in France. France was humiliated and remained isolated for twenty-three years, while Germany built up a group of alliances to protect her all-dominant position in Europe.

This period witnessed the arrival of the common man and the awakened subject nations, the rise in the standard of living, the spread of political suffrage, mass production, and world prices in agricultural commodities. All these began rapidly to transform Europe. When William II dropped his pilot, Bismarck, in 1890,—and that meant the end of the German-Russian alliance,—the Franco-Russian alliance was formed (in 1893) to balance the German domination. The principle of balance of power began to function, with its ever shifting adjustment and ominous possibilities of war. The protective tariff adopted by Germany in 1879, after the example of the United States, began the growth of economic nationalism on a large scale in Europe.

Nations which came late in the race for a place in the sun, especially Germany, Italy, and Japan, maneuvered for position on the chessboard. And they, be it noted, were and are only the vanguard of others yet to come.

The key to the prewar situation in Europe was then, as it is now, in Germany. The central fact was the industrialization, by about 1890, of Germany, the first state to be so transformed on the Continent. Germany, though still the dominant continental power, became a world power with world-wide commercial interests. It formulated a world policy. It felt the disadvantage of coming late in the race for world markets and colonies; of the smallness of its own market, which could not begin to absorb the products of its industrial equipment; of its geographical situation with reference to the seas menaced by England; and of its continental alliances matched by balance of power through France and Russia and later England. This led to a truculent foreign policy, aggressive and challenging—challenging England in the world at large and in the Near East in particular, and France and Russia on the Continent, and the latter also in the Near East. In addition to this, step by step, the failure to solve problems of nationalism in Austria-Hungary and in the Balkans, as well as in Germany, and of world economy in the making, led to the World War.

THE WORLD WAR AND THE PEACE SETTLEMENTS

While it may be rightly maintained that Germany and Austria were mainly responsible for the immediate outbreak of the World War, few informed scholars would deny that all nations concerned shared in that responsibility. That war was not only a cascade of thrones and empires; it was also a gigantic upheaval of political, economic, social, and cultural forces. It completely upset what appeared at that time to be the balance of forces. It exhausted not only material resources to an extent of some 340 billions of dollars and millions of lives, but it also uprooted the moorings of our common civilization, created mountains of debts, devastated northern France, Belgium, Serbia, and Poland (without touching in that way an inch of German soil), and left Germany humiliated, filled with hatred. The humiliation of Germany, more than the great losses sustained through the Treaty of Versailles, was to form thereafter the motive force of postwar years. A great nation, like a fallen aviator, must seek to come back, to regain its nerve, to justify itself. The peace treaties would have had to be divine to have calmed the angry forces which the World War generated.

We cannot here enter into the details of peacemaking, although certain dominant items will find elucidation hereafter. In line with the force of nationalism the German, Austro-Hungarian, Russian, and Turkish empires foundered and their subject peoples revolted. After the revolution, Russia emerged as the Union of Soviet Socialist Republics, proclaiming a new social order, Communism, which met with abject failure by 1921. New nations appeared from the ruins of the fallen empires. The British empire continued its devolution into a Commonwealth of Nations.[8] The League of Nations attempted to bind all nations together as the only way out of a politically disintegrating world. It had to take the world as it was. The time was just the worst possible for starting such an experiment.

---

[8] Statute of Westminster, 1931, in 22 Geo. 5, c. 4, *Complete Statutes of England,* Vol. XXIV, p. 125.

THE POSTWAR PERIOD

The war was fought on both sides with an astounding degree of economic coöperation, thus working in line with the force of economic interdependency and accelerating the speed with which it was already working. But this coöperation was abruptly abandoned at the time of the armistice, with harmful results. Each nation was thereby encouraged to struggle singlehandedly, and this resulted in a virulent economic nationalism after the war. German wealth abroad was seized and an impossible load of reparations (after a tragic delay) was imposed upon Germany, alongside of the impossible load of Inter-Allied and Allied debts to the United States. The increasing reaction against economic interdependency brought a crop of high tariffs, quotas, subsidies, and other measures. Soviet Russia was among the first to apply the policy of complete economic nationalism, owing to the monopoly of foreign trade by the State.

In such a world of closing markets, Germany, saddled down with an impossible debt and an already half-inflated currency when the war closed in 1918, became a victim of complete inflation in 1923.[4] The attempt to rescue Germany so as to get at least reparations and to fund debts led step by step through the Dawes and the Young plans in 1924 and 1930 and to the complete wreckage of the entire debt and monetary structure in the World Depression beginning in 1929.[5]

---

[4] Reinhold, Peter P., *The Economic, Financial and Political State of Germany since the War* (New Haven, 1918); Siegfried, André, *Europe's Crisis* (New York, 1936).

[5] Wheeler-Bennett, John W., *The Wreck of Reparations* (New York, 1933), pp. 255 ff.

To have worked in line to adjust and balance the two forces of nationalism and economic interdependency would have required a wide-reaching program of international coöperation in politics and economics for which no nation was then prepared. It would have required such sacrifices as to seem too great for the times. That the Depression has cost each nation much more is self-evident, but no one had the courage to demand sacrifices of that scope. It would have called for the lowering, instead of the raising, of tariffs; the reopening of old markets and the opening of new ones; the all-around drastic scaling-down of intergovernmental and private debts to capacity-to-pay figures; the access of Great Powers without colonies to raw materials based on open markets without tariffs and on sound and equitable international exchange;[6] disarmament; treaty adjustments made in a friendly spirit; and a strong League of Nations of all states.

These were some of the reasons why the World Depression came on and paid such a long and decisive visit. World trade diminished to at least one-half of its previous volume, the wealth of countries was deflated by often as much as two-thirds, and unemployment ranged at one time between thirty and fifty millions.[7] The Depression brought economic nationalism to its highest development. Trade in many places became, in large part, barter. Through this policy the nations

---

[6] Patterson, Ernest Minor, *The World's Economic Dilemma* (New York, 1930); Salter, Sir Arthur, *Recovery, the Second Effort* (New York, 1932).

[7] *The Course and Phases of the World Economic Depression:* Report Presented to the League of Nations (2 vols.; Geneva, 1931 ff.); *World Economic Survey*, III year, 1933–34 (League of Nations, Geneva, 1934); *Review of World Trade, 1933* (League of Nations, Geneva, 1934 ff.).

tried to recover, separately, by raising themselves by their own bootstraps. The limit of such a policy—a falling standard of living—reached its breaking point in Japan in 1931 when the Manchurian episode was begun, in Italy in 1935 when Abyssinia was assaulted, and in . . . we will pause to let history write in the name of the next country, if these problems are not resolutely attacked.

The unsolved problems of the World War and the chaos of the World Depression reached a bottom in 1932 and 1933. Whether this was the only bottom, or is only the first bottom, will probably depend upon at least two things: the ability of statesmen to transform the partial and temporary recovery due to economic nationalism based on economic war into a complete world-wide recovery based on international economic peace, and a similar ability to check the ravages of opposed political, social, and national entities through international organization, limitation and reduction of armaments, and the creation of an international political organization able to conciliate and adjust international conflicts.

The year 1933 witnessed the failures of the World Economic Conference and the Disarmament Conference. The World Economic Conference was sprung chiefly on the inability of Great Britain and the United States to agree on the relative values of the pound and the dollar. The United States refused to give the British an advantage in the markets of the world by allowing them to keep the pound anywhere between 5 and 15 per cent below the old level of $4.87.[8] The Disarmament Conference struck the rocks with the advent of Hitler to

---

[8] Delaisi, Francis, *La Bataille de l'Or* (Paris, 1933), pp. 70–131.

power in Germany and the resultant fear of aggressive unilateral action, as well as the inability of the armed Powers
to translate into concrete terms the phrase "equality of rights
to Germany in a system of security."[9] This happened in the
atmosphere of the challenge of Japan to freely signed treaties
and to the international settlement of disputes exhibited by
Japanese policy in the Manchurian episode. The demand to
revise the peace treaties by threats, instead of by free and voluntary negotiation, was not calculated to improve conditions.
Rejecting the negotiation of either disarmament by other
Powers, or its own rearmament, Germany left the League in
October, 1933, and proceeded to arm and to revise the Treaty
of Versailles unilaterally.

The persecution of the Jews and the reversal of relations
with the Soviet Union increased the tension. It was thought,
however, that Germany's success in the Saar plebiscite in
January, 1935, might afford an atmosphere in which something might be done. In 1934, France apparently decided
against a preventive war on the Hitler régime and under
Barthou began a diplomatic offensive to create a series of
regional mutual-assistance pacts to prepare the ground for
the time when serious disarmament might take place. With
Hitler on the horizon, France considered its system of alliances inadequate, especially after the Polish-German Pact of
January, 1934. England gave the idea of regional security
moral support and urged the Eastern Pact proposal, with its

---

[9] Wheeler-Bennett, John W., *Disarmament and Security since Locarno,
1925–31* (London, 1932); *idem, The Pipe Dream of Peace: The Story of the
Collapse of Disarmament* (New York, 1935).

Franco-Soviet Pact supplement, upon Germany.[10] So on February 3, 1935, England and France announced an agreement which declared for equality of rights to Germany in a system of security and for the negotiation of an Eastern Pact on the model of the Pact of Locarno, a Western Air Pact, as well as a Danubian Pact, which was to be negotiated chiefly through Mussolini, who in January had made the famous Franco-Italian agreement with Laval.[11]

Germany replied in a vague friendly way, stressing only its interest in the Air Pact. Sir John Simon and Anthony Eden had arranged to visit Berlin for preliminary negotiations to carry out the London Agreement, when on March 16, 1935, Germany unilaterally began the abrogation of the military, naval, and air provisions of the Treaty of Versailles.[12] This brought the French negotiations for an Eastern Pact (of Germany, Russia, Poland, Czechoslovakia, Finland, Estonia, Latvia, and Lithuania) to a standstill and resulted in an agreement in principle to the terms of a Franco-Soviet pact of mutual assistance on April 10.[13]

At the Stresa Conference of Treaty Powers on April 11-14, and the meeting of the Council of the League of Nations, April 15-17, Germany was declared a violator of the Treaty

[10] Great Britain, Foreign Office, *Correspondence Showing the Course of Certain Diplomatic Discussions Directed towards Securing an European Settlement, June 1934 to March 1936*, Miscellaneous, No. 3 (1936), Cmd. 5143.

[11] *Ibid.*, pp. 15-17. See also *Völkerbund, The Disarmament Conference: Journal of the German Association for League of Nations Questions* (Wilhelm Schaer, ed.; Geneva, 1932 ff.), Nos. 104, 111-112, 161-163 (hereafter cited as *Völkerbund*). Apparently in close touch with the German Foreign Office for which it carries on propaganda. Useful for the publication of documents.

[12] *Völkerbund*, No. 123.   [13] *Ibid.*, No. 138.

of Versailles; no action, however, not even sanctions, followed. It was on April 13, when fear of action by the Powers was uppermost in Hitler's mind, that Germany agreed to negotiate an Eastern nonaggression pact "with the Powers interested in Eastern European questions," even though at the same time certain signatory Powers might conclude mutual-assistance pacts.[14] Under these conditions, Soviet Russia and France signed their Pact of Mutual Assistance within the framework of the League and supplementary to the Locarno Pact on May 2.[15] On May 16, Soviet Russia and Czechoslovakia signed a similar pact. Hitler, in an address on May 21, declared Germany's readiness to take part in a system of collective coöperation, but regarded it as essential in such an event to take the law of perpetual development into account by keeping open the possibilities of treaty revisions.[16] Germany charged that the Franco-Soviet Pact violated the Pact of Locarno. This interpretation was rejected in separate notes by France on June 25, by England on July 5, by Italy on July 15, and by Belgium on July 19. At the end of July, 1935, Germany announced that she "was obliged to maintain her objections to the Franco-Soviet Pact and that she could not consider the matter settled."[17]

In the meanwhile, Mussolini, hard pressed in domestic policy, had decided that there was still time before war took place in Europe to create a Fascist empire by acquiring Abyssinia. We need not recount in detail the menace to Britain's

---

[14] *Ibid.*

[15] *International Conciliation*, April, 1936, pamphlet No. 319.

[16] *Völkerbund*, Nos. 155–157.　　[17] *Ibid.*, Nos. 153–154.

imperial communications and her sudden interest in positive
and effective collective action, or France's plight in her effort
to save the Franco-Italian Agreement of January, 1935, and
give Hitler no excuse for another unilateral action. That the
League went to the extent of its powers and that collective
action might even have failed because of the lack of human
experience with this mode of action, requiring sacrifices by
all Powers in whatever way concerned, whether politically,
commercially, or socially, is all too evident. The key to it all
was supplied in two episodes: the Anglo-French negotiations
and the neutrality legislation enacted by the United States.

The Anglo-French negotiations are exposed in two published documents, the communications of Sir Samuel Hoare,
British Minister for Foreign Affairs, and M. Corbin, French
Ambassador in London, September 26 and October 5, 1935.[18]
In the first of these documents Sir Samuel outlines British
policy in answer to a question by France in connection with
the dispute between Italy and Abyssinia, concerning how far
the French "might be assured in the future of the immediate
and effective application by [England] of all sanctions provided in Article XVI of the Covenant in the event of a violation of the Covenant of the League of Nations and a resort
to force in Europe," especially "on the part of some European
state, whether or not that state might be a member of the

---

[18] Great Britain, Foreign Office, *Dispute between Ethiopia and Italy: Correspondence in Connection with the Application of Article XVI of the Covenant
of the League of Nations,* January, 1936 (Ethiopia, No. 2, 1936), Cmd. 5072;
*Dispute between Ethiopia and Italy: Co-ordination of Measures under Ar-
ticle XVI* . . . Geneva, February 12, 1936 (Ethiopia, No. 3, 1936), Cmd. 5094;
London *Times,* September 30, October 8, 1935; also *Völkerbund,* No. 142.

League of Nations." England was leading the movement to impose sanctions on Italy, and France wanted to know whether, if she agreed to their application against Italy, England in the same way would agree to their application against Germany in a future transgression—possibly the abrogation of the Locarno Pact.

Sir Samuel directed attention to his speech in the League Assembly on September 14 in which he declared that the United Kingdom

would be second to none in their intention to fulfill, within the measure of their capacity the obligations which the Covenant lays upon them. . . . I added that to suggest or insinuate that this policy was for some reason peculiar to the Italo-Abyssinian conflict would be a complete misunderstanding . . . any other view would at once be an underestimate of British good faith and an imputation upon British sincerity. . . . The country stands for collective maintenance of the Covenant in its entirety and particularly for steady and collective resistance to all acts of unprovoked aggression.

It is at once evident that procedure under Article XVI of the Covenant, appropriate as regards a positive act of unprovoked aggression, is not made applicable as regards the negative act of the failure to fulfill the terms of a treaty. Further, in the case of a resort to force, it is clear that there may be degrees of culpability and degrees of aggression, and that consequently, in cases where Article XVI applies, the nature of the action appropriate to be taken under it may vary according to the circumstances of each particular case.

And similarly in regard to treaty obligations it is pertinent to recall that, as I have already said at Geneva, elasticity is a part of security, and that every member of the League must recognize, as the Covenant itself recognizes, that the world is not static.

The government, so ran the document, will firmly hold to this policy "so long as the League remains an effective body." "If risks for peace are to be run they must be run by all."

The conclusion is obvious: in the language of *The Cat and the Fiddle,* England did not say yes, England did not say no. It wished to reserve its independence of action. But this was in reality a negative answer.

Sir Samuel asked the French government the question whether England could count on French support where

a member of the League of Nations, who declares himself ready to fulfill his obligations in accordance with the terms of Article 16 of the Covenant and who is making the necessary preparations to that end, should be attacked before the Article in question became applicable, that is to say, before the other members of the League of Nations were expressly bound to lend this member the mutual support provided for against a Covenant-breaking state.

The French government replied:

The proposal of the British Government, if given a wide application, fills in very opportunely a gap in the system of "collective security" to which our two governments are firmly attached.

The obligation of assistance which is contemplated, binding the two Governments, must be reciprocal, that is to say, it must bind Great Britain with regard to France as much as France with regard to Great Britain.

Moreover, it would be difficult to imagine that a state might or might not be regarded as having been attacked, according to whether the attacks occurred on land, by sea, or in the air. The undertaking of assistance must therefore operate in each and every one of these cases.

Finally, the mutual support from now on provided for in the

third paragraph of Article 16 is equally due in case, in virtue of Article 17, Article 16 is applied. The preliminary assistance which the British Government proposes must therefore be equally assured whether the aggressor State is or is not a member of the League of Nations.

In a general way the contemplated undertaking ought to take effect only after a joint investigation has been made into the circumstances and agreement reached on the measures of precaution which these circumstances may justify as being strictly necessary in order to prepare for the carrying out of the Council's ultimate recommendations. This joint investigation ought to take place as soon as a state of political tension arises sufficiently serious to give ground for fear lest it lead sooner or later to the applications of Articles 16 and 17.

Subject to these observations and on condition of reciprocity, I am authorized to inform your Excellency that the French Government is ready to assume in regard to his Majesty's Government the following undertakings:

(*a*) If either of the two Powers judges it necessary to take military, naval or air measures, with a view to placing itself in a position to carry out, in case of need, its obligations of assistance arising out of the Covenant of the League of Nations or the Treaties of Locarno, it will enter into consultation on this subject with the other Power; the procedure shall be similar if either of the two Powers judges it necessary to take military, naval or air measures, with a view to placing itself in a position to meet, should it arise, a situation in which, under the Covenant of the League of Nations or the Treaties of Locarno, it would be entitled to receive the assistance of the other Power.

(*b*) The fact that one or other of the two Powers, after this consultation and the resulting agreement, takes the measures referred to above shall not on that account be regarded as constituting a provocation such as would justify any failure by a third State to fulfill its international obligations.

(*c*) If either of the two Powers is attacked on account of such measures taken after consultation and agreement, the other Power will render it assistance.

In this document transmitted by M. Corbin, France indicated its terms for its support in the Italo-Abyssinian conflict. They were a binding promise by England, should the danger of a German violation arise, to consult beforehand and give assistance.

Mussolini knew that he could safely go ahead, and he did so within a week, since France would say it would fulfill the Covenant, of course, in its minimum terms, as long as England would not interpret the Pact of Locarno and the Covenant in an effective manner with respect to Germany. Interesting as this must have been to Mussolini, it was still more interesting to Hitler. It told him that if the Italo-Ethiopian conflict really became serious, he could violate the Pact of Locarno without fear of a reply by force.

Another reason for the failure of collective action was our neutrality legislation of August 31, 1935, which forbade the sale to all belligerents of implements of war, but not the raw materials of war such as oil, cotton, copper, and the like— that is, it permitted a neutrality with profits, in this instance favoring the aggressor.[19] It will be remembered that, in 1933, Mr. Norman Davis announced at the Disarmament Conference what would occur should a disarmament treaty be made.

---

[19] 48 *Statutes at Large,* p. 1104; also *Public Resolution* No. 74, 74th Congress (H. J. Res. 491), approved February 29, 1936, and Department of State, *Press Releases,* March 7, 1936, p. 168. See also Jessup, Deak, Phillips, and Reede, *Neutrality, Its History, Economics and Law* (4 vols.; New Haven, 1935–36).

Recognising that any breach or threat of breach of the Pact of Paris [the Briand-Kellogg Pact] is a matter of concern to all the signatories thereto, the Government of the United States of America declares that, in the event of a breach or threat of breach of this Pact, it will be prepared to confer with a view to the maintenance of peace in the event that consultation for such purpose is arranged pursuant to Articles . . . and . . . of Part I of the Disarmament Convention. In the event that a decision is taken by a conference of the Powers in consultation, in determining the aggressor, with which, on the basis of its independent judgment, the Government of the United States agreed, the Government of the United States will undertake to refrain from any action and to withhold protection from its citizens if engaged in activities which would tend to defeat the collective effort which the States in consultation might have decided upon against the aggressor.[20]

The neutrality legislation did not prevent consultation, but it did prevent the United States from taking any action, except to observe strict neutrality, in its trade with the belligerents equally. It is true that the present administration endeavored, by the pressure of public opinion, to keep the trade with Italy down to normal prewar limits and thus take the profits out of neutrality. But its efficacy remains to be seen. Whether as an excuse or as the real reason, sanctions on oil were not applied, and according to British statistics our exports of oil to Italy far exceeded those made on the prewar basis.[21]

Collective action really failed not because it could not possibly have succeeded in this situation, but because three Great

---

[20] *Records of the Conference for the Reduction and Limitation of Armaments, Series B: Minutes of the General Commission* (League of Nations, Geneva, 1933), Vol. II, pp. 475, 495, May 22, 24, 1933.

[21] Sir John Simon in the House of Commons, June 23, 1936. *International Conciliation,* September, 1936, pamphlet No. 322, p. 391.

Powers could not agree to make it effective. They had it in their power to do so. This reminds us why it was impossible to disarm. Each nation would give up only what would injure it if used by a hostile neighbor against it. Each nation wanted to have its cake and to eat it too.

Statesmen immediately made the requisite deductions, and armaments were pushed forward with feverish energy. When the Italo-Ethiopian situation, as well as Germany's internal condition, reached a critical stage, Hitler suddenly acted on March 7, 1936, by sending armed forces into the demilitarized Rhine zone, thus violating the Pact of Locarno. He gave as his excuse that the Franco-Soviet Pact, which passed the French Chamber of Deputies on February 27 and was certain of ratification thereafter, violated the Locarno Pact.

For a moment, Hitler feared a preventive war by France, but finally the decision was taken there to await collective action on the part of Locarno Powers. The stand of England was a keen disappointment to those who believed in collective action, although it was easily predictable from the documents of September and October, 1935, cited above. Germany was declared a violator of the Pact of Locarno. Staff consultations were held, against the eventuality of any act of armed aggression against France or Belgium.[22] The peace plan of Hitler, in his address of March 7, 1936, was nevertheless taken into consideration under British pressure with the understanding that questions were to be asked to elucidate it.

---

[22] Great Britain, Foreign Office, *Correspondence with the German Government regarding the German Proposals for an European Settlement, March 24–May 6, 1936,* Miscellaneous, No. 6 (1936), Cmd. 5175; see also Cmd. 5134, 5194.

In his address[23] Hitler stated: "We have no territorial demands to make in Europe." "We, too, smart under the fact that the access to sea of a nation of thirty-three millions [Poland] leads through former Reich territory, but we recognize that it would be as unreasonable as it is impossible simply to deny access to the sea to such a great state." Were these slips of the tongue, or were they his assurance that the territorial boundaries, as fixed in Europe by the Treaty of Versailles, were accepted by Hitler, and that demands for revision thereafter would not include these? Then could an Eastern Pact be signed, if Hitler should agree to the eastern boundaries?

In the questionnaire of May 6,[24] transmitted by Eden, the basic question asked was: "Is Germany now in a position to conclude genuine treaties? It is of course clear that negotiations for a treaty would be useless, if one of the parties here-

---

[23] *Völkerbund*, Nos. 153–154; also *International Conciliation*, No. 319. It should be noted that he pictured Germany's chief grievance as follows: "It was that unreason which was applied with scientific method to Germany, a nation of sixty-five millions; first, all possible vital links with the outer world were cut off, all economic connections robbed, all capital abroad confiscated, trade annihilated; then this nation was saddled with an unbelievable debt of astronomic proportions; then foreign credits were given so that this debt might be paid, and in order to pay the interest on those credits, exportation had to be forced at any cost; finally, our export markets were walled up, and thus this nation was driven into terrible poverty and misery, and then accused of incapacity to pay and of bad will. And that was called 'wise statesmanship.'" Note how closely this follows the reasoning of Clemenceau's answer to Lloyd George's Memorandum of March 25, 1919, at the Peace Conference (Nitti, Francesco, *The Wreck of Europe* [Indianapolis, 1922], pp. 91–105). Clemenceau prophetically pointed out what, in the peace terms, would really hurt Germany more—namely, those advantages which would accrue chiefly to England. For Hitler's other addresses in March, 1936, see *Völkerbund*, Nos. 155–157.

[24] Cmd. 5175.

after felt free to deny its obligations on the ground that that party was not in a condition to conclude a binding treaty." And referring to the express distinction drawn by Hitler between the Reich and the German nation, the questionnaire went on to say: "A distinction is apparently drawn between the Reich and the German nation. The question is really whether Germany now considers that a point has been reached at which she can signify that she recognizes and intends to respect the existing territorial and political status of Europe, except in so far as this might be subsequently modified by free negotiation and agreement."

No answer to this fundamental issue has yet been given. Perhaps Hitler plans to give it by acts, not words. The demand for colonies has become insistent. A gentlemen's agreement has been made by him with Mussolini in respect to a hands-off policy in Austria. Hitler in 1935 promised noninterference in the internal affairs of Austria, as well as nonaggression against her. Is the bilateral Austro-German Pact of July, 1936, an answer to the questonnaire on noninterference, as well as on nonaggression? The Powers are interested in a multilateral pact on this matter, not merely a deal between Hitler and Mussolini tenable at their mercurial pleasure.

Equality in armament may be a load too heavy for Germany to carry in its present financial condition, but it is the price of its insistent demands. Evidently there must be a steady increase in its armaments, as its fearful neighbors always retaliate by proportionate increases.

The Spanish revolution has illustrated the feeble structure on which hangs the peace of the world. Actually the next world war may be said to have begun, if that war, which can hardly be identified as a civil war, involves others. Ordinarily, such a conflict would have been settled within Spain's borders. But today the social causes of a future world war have been brought to the fore. These have their roots in the Bolsheviks' dream that their state would be the first state in a world Union of Soviet Socialist Republics. Such a union, they believed, would come about as a result of social revolutions which would end and follow the World War. In this they were as bitterly disappointed as they were in trying to create a Communist state. Caught now in the midst of "building socialism" (not Communism) "in a single state" and between Fascist Japan dominant in the Far East and a rearmed and aggressive Nazi Germany in Europe, they have been working aggressively to prevent the outbreak of a world war. Such a war would involve the Soviet Union on at least two fronts, if not three, and put in question even the present socialistic experiment, which appears to be driven constantly to the right by the two historical forces we have analyzed.

In 1926–28, when Stalin became supreme over Trotsky, the Third International entered a decline.[25] Thereafter, the dominant Bolshevik institution was to be the Soviet Union and not the Third International. Membership in the League of Nations, the signing of mutual assistance pacts to ward off the German danger, the recent trial against the Trotsky adherents in Russia, as well as the policy of the United Front (a proof of Bolshevik weakness), all are signs pointing in the

---

[25] Florinsky, Michael T., *World Revolution and the U. S. S. R.* (New York, 1933); Trotsky, Leon, *The Third International after Lenin* (New York, 1936).

same direction.[26] The Third International has become more of a liability than an asset to the Bolsheviks. Yet they hang on to it, doubtless more for internal consumption and for reasons of "face." It could be an asset only if a second world war were followed by social revolutions—but, then, a second world war might crumble the Soviet Union.

The Bolshevik menace has never been taken very seriously by the statesmen of Europe. It was used conveniently by Mussolini and Hitler to climb into power. But now that Hitler and Mussolini have raised the social revolution as an issue in European politics by aggressive action in Spain, it is in order to ask whether they are more interested in strategic considerations and world power than in the fate of society in that country. Is not Hitler more interested in getting world approbation for the old German policy of either controlling Russia or breaking it up because the reëstablishment of Russia as a world power, whether Tsarist, Liberal, or Bolshevik, in Europe and Asia means the inability of Germany to dominate Europe and of Japan to dominate the Far East? Those who know thoroughly Bismarck's policy of controlling Russia, as well as the meaning of the Treaty of Brest-Litovsk of March, 1918, when Germany separated the Ukraine from Bolshevik Russia in order to dominate Europe, as well as that granary of the world, can answer the question adequately. After all, it was the German government that transported the Bolshevik leaders from Switzerland in a sealed train across Germany early in 1917 so as to have the kind of revoluton

---

[26] *Verbatim Report of the Negotiations between the 2nd and 3rd Internationals on the Question of Supporting the Spanish Workers* (London, Modern Books Ltd., 1935).

that would put Russia out of the war, and a German brand of peace which would secure Germany's domination in Europe and probably in the world.[27]

The attempt to make Europe and the world the scene of a conflict between Bolshevism and Fascism or Naziism is at best heavy-laden with imperial strategy and the struggle for world power. The fact is that there is little difference between Soviet Russia, Nazi Germany, and Fascist Italy with respect to despotism, and doubtless there will be little in the future in respect to their form of society. For Hitler and Mussolini are advancing and must advance to the left. This is amply demonstrated by Mussolini's recent decrees and by Hitler's recent speech at Nuremberg. Will the near future see a cascade of doctrines as the past saw a cascade of thrones and empires after the World War?

Hitler's recent "if I had the Urals" speech is important not only in view of what has been said above, but even more in respect to internal conditions. After nearly four years Hitler has not been able to raise the standard of living. Moreover, he has been forced to adopt a four-year plan à la Bolshevik with the object of making Germany self-supporting—synthetically at least, if not otherwise.[28] He is begging the German people to be patient. The magic National Socialist formula has not worked. Bolshevik planning and regimentation must be adopted to save Germany. What will become of private capitalism in Germany and Italy as the dictators are driven

---

[27] Hoffmann, Major-General Max, *War Diaries and Other Papers* (2 vols.; London, 1929), Vol. II, p. 176.

[28] New York *Times*, September 10, 1936.

ever to the left by the historical forces noted above? The
issue, then, is not that Hitler and Mussolini are saving and
will save capitalism for the world.[29] The chances are excellent
that they will bury it. Capitalism can and will be saved only
by intelligent democracies through sane social reform and
not by stupid dictatorships with their planned societies.

We have come now to the end of our survey of present-day
Europe. We have seen conditions growing steadily worse and
pointing definitely to a second world war with world-wide
inflation and social upheaval as its possibilities. Man has failed
to balance and adjust the two contradictory forces of nationalism, which often conceals the mask of imperialism, and of
economic interdependency. No one individual in power, no
nation, no class is willing to sacrifice except for immediate
material interests.

One or two faint hopes brighten the horizon. The American reciprocity agreements and the Tripartite Monetary
Agreement give hope that, if used intelligently, they may begin a reversal of the trends indicated above.[30] May it be so!
Another hope has been kindled in the Balkans and the Near
East through the Balkan Conferences and the Balkan Entente. This regional agreement, incomplete as it is, made pos-

[29] Since this lecture was delivered, both Hitler and Mussolini have confirmed
this statement. See especially Anne O'Hare McCormick's interview with
Mussolini (New York *Times,* February 2, 1937) in which he is reported to
have said: "I tell you democracy is only a mask for capitalism which clings
desperately to outmoded forms that allowed it free play. The era of capitalism
is over. Here in Italy it is finished, it is dead. If by democracy you mean government for and in the interests of the people then our system and ours alone
is truly democratic." Note that he omitted the phrase "by the people."

[30] *Ibid.,* September 30–October 2, 1936.

sible the revision of the Peace Treaty of Lausanne at the recently called Montreux Conference. The clauses on the demilitarization and passage of the Straits were revised.[31] Mussolini and Hitler were given a public reprimand, thereby, that treaties may be revised peacefully. This has added momentum to the regional treatment of the problems of security.

To those who know the foreign policy of the United States, it is no secret that confusion and danger of war in Europe complicate the situation, in fact, produce new problems for us on the Pacific and in the Far East.[32]

As a nation we fervently want peace. The practical issue before us is whether our neutrality legislation and the foreign policy permitted by it will keep us out of war. To believe that the existing situation in Europe and Asia can be met successfully by each nation's retaining its freedom of action or isolation is to court disaster. The best way, after all, to stay out of war is to prevent war.

It was neutrality which involved the United States in two out of the three wars that it has had with European nations. Its present policy, which permits profits out of the miseries of others and prevents others from settling their quarrels, may involve it in war for the defense of neutral rights. A suddenly applied policy of complete political and economic isolation might lead to a vast internal catastrophe and social upheaval.

---

[31] Kerner and Howard, *The Balkan Conferences and the Balkan Entente, 1930–35* (Berkeley, 1936), and Howard, Harry N., "The Straits after the Montreux Conference" (*Foreign Affairs,* October, 1936).

[32] Stimson, Henry L., *The Far Eastern Crisis* (New York, 1936), and Pearson and Brown, *The American Diplomatic Game* (New York, 1935), enumerate many instances of this.

A policy of complete coöperation with the League, or an Association of Nations reformed to suit us, is for us today an academic question.[33] There remains at present one policy: it is that of limited and adjustable coöperation, whereby the United States would consult with other nations, and whereby, if we agreed in the designation of the aggressor, we would do nothing to prevent others from settling the quarrel. It may be that such a policy could prevent war if it were known beforehand that the United States had such a policy and that it might be used against an aggressor. We might be able to remain out of such a conflict and even retain our freedom of action, and might also be able to act in the interests of peace for ourselves and for the world at large.

---

[33] See the platforms of the Democratic and Republican parties in this campaign. Shotwell, J. T., *On the Rim of the Abyss* (New York, 1936), is an able presentation of the most effective way of dealing with this problem.

THE UNITED STATES IN WORLD TRADE: AN OUTLINE

HENRY F. GRADY

PROFESSOR OF INTERNATIONAL TRADE
IN THE UNIVERSITY OF CALIFORNIA

Lecture delivered October 14, 1936

THE UNITED STATES IN WORLD TRADE: AN OUTLINE

TRENDS IN AMERICAN FOREIGN TRADE

THE OUTSTANDING FACTOR affecting the trend in the development of American foreign trade has been the growth of industrialism in the United States. Before the World War, our export trade was of importance mainly to agriculture. Prior to 1900, agricultural products accounted for two-thirds of the total value of our exports. Just prior to the World War, the exports of agricultural and nonagricultural products were about even. But from 1929 to 1931, nonagricultural exports represented about two-thirds of the total. This change in the composition of our export trade has its counterpart in the movement of population from the farms to the cities. This does not mean, of course, that the growth of industrialization in the United States has made agriculture any less dependent upon foreign trade. Large percentages of our agricultural crops are still produced for foreign markets and the respective demands for raw materials and foodstuffs by domestic industries and domestic workers depend in large measure upon the foreign demand for American manufactures.

There are, however, other factors which in part account for the declining importance of agricultural products, especially foodstuffs, in our export trade and indicate that the American producers of foodstuffs will continue to rely more heavily in the future on the domestic market. These are the development of large-scale agriculture in Canada, Argentina, Australia, and New Zealand, which has been made possible by machinery and scientific agriculture, import restrictions imposed by European countries in an effort to produce their own food supplies, and the increased demand abroad for heavy-industry goods which are required for the industrial development necessary to those countries which are seeking economic self-sufficiency.

The effect on American agriculture is in the direction of greater diversification. Our food production will consist more and more of a larger proportion of perishable and semiperishable products, such as dairy products, fruits, and vegetables. Thus it may be seen how science and invention, economic conditions abroad, and foreign commercial policy are affecting the economic development of the United States.

The change in the composition of our export trade is reflected also in a change in the destination of that trade. Although Europe is by far the greatest market, it has declined in relative importance in the last fifty years, and Canada, Asia, and South America have risen in importance. Whereas formerly the United States was important to Europe mainly as a source of raw materials for manufacture and food for an industrial population, it is now Europe's chief competitor in the industrial markets of the world. We are therefore much more concerned than we used to be about the economic policies of European nations toward other countries of the world, particularly those in Asia and South America. The nature of the commercial relations existing between the industrial countries of western Europe and the nonindustrial countries of eastern Europe are of vital significance to us. We are directly affected by the growth of the preferential system within the British empire. We observe with anxiety the recent development of bilateral trade balancing implemented by exchange control, clearing agreements, import quotas, trade monopolies, and the like. Under those conditions, the principle of the most-favored-nation treatment has a new significance in the commercial relations of the United States.

The growth of our export trade in the last seventy-five years is accounted for in large part by commodities which were not in existence in 1860 or were relatively unimportant in our production at that time. These are mainly in machinery (including agricultural machinery), electrical devices, automobiles, and a long list of chemicals, nonferrous metals, and certain types of food products. At the beginning of the nineteenth century, the United Kingdom was the undisputed leader in machinery production. By 1913, Germany was the leading exporter of machinery, followed closely by the United Kingdom and the United States. By 1929, the United States was far in the lead. The machinery industry in the United States has been particularly favored by the factors making possible large-scale production. It is now the leading American manufacturing industry. In 1900, the textile industry was first in rank, machinery ranking only fourth, but by 1929 machinery was in the lead. The supremacy of the United States in the world markets for machinery is due to a number of factors, one being a large domestic demand resulting from the high level of wages in this country, and another, the relatively large supply of capital and cheap raw materials.

The change in the composition of our import trade has been the converse of that in the export trade. There has been a decline in the proportion accounted for by manufactures which we now produce ourselves, and a rise in the relative importance of crude materials for our industries and certain foodstuffs which, for the most part, are not grown in the United States. During the years from 1830 to 1860, the relative positions of the various components of the industrial structure remained about the same, but after 1860, with the growth of industrialization in both the United States and Europe, Europe continued to have need of our raw materials and food products, but we needed less and less of Europe's manufactures, and as our need for raw materials became more diversified we began to compete with Europe for them in the world markets. From 1821 to 1860, Europe supplied the United States with from 61 to 71 per cent of its imports, consisting of such goods as cottons, woolens, linens, laces, iron and steel products, earthenware, silks, wines, fruits, and furs. In late years, when crude materials and foodstuffs have accounted for as much as 57 per cent of our total imports, less than 30 per cent of the total has been supplied by Europe, and Asia, Canada, and Latin America have supplied an increasing proportion.

The American demand for raw materials is not only more intense than it used to be, but also more varied. Such items as nickel, tin, antimony, tungsten, manganese, and vanadium were not found in our import trade in 1860. In 1929, more than 30 per cent of our total imports were of a sort demanded by industries not in existence a half-century ago; for example, rubber, jute, tin, wood pulp, raw silk, crude petroleum, and various gums, balsams, resins, oil seeds, and vegetable oils.

"Due sometimes to localization of certain industrial plants within the United States and sometimes to lower production costs abroad, and to the need for specific kinds of minerals, we often import considerable quantities of the same class of products of which we have large resources at home. For example, in 1929 we imported over 3,000,000 tons of iron ore and concentrates, 380,000 tons of crude bauxite,—the mineral from which aluminum is obtained,—180,000 tons of copper ores and concentrates, 79,000,000 barrels of crude petroleum, to say nothing of the manufactures of these various materials."[1] Similar observations might be made with respect to animals, meat products, dairy products, vegetables, fruit, sugar, vegetable oils and seeds, nursery products, raw cotton, wool, and others.

THE POSITION OF THE UNITED STATES IN INTERNATIONAL FINANCE

The industrial rise of the United States has been accompanied by changes not only in its foreign trade but also in its position in international finance. Before the World War, the United States was a debtor nation. It had used European capital to construct its railway system, begun in about 1830 and rapidly expanded in the latter half of the century, and to exploit the new resources which the railways made available, and to build factories to take advantage of the domestic market which the railways had greatly enlarged. During the third quarter of the nineteenth century, from 1850 to 1875, the United States had regularly an unfavorable balance of

---

[1] Isaac Lippincott, *The Development of Modern World Trade* (1936), p. 85.

trade, for the money which Europe lent to, and invested in, our enterprises was in effect spent in Europe and imported into the United States in the form of transportation and industrial equipment. Later, when the payments owed to Europe for interest and dividends accruing from the loans and investments and as the result of liquidation of the loans and the gradual transfer of ownership of American industries to Americans exceeded new loans and investments from abroad, the balance of trade became favorable and thus the earnings from, as well as the repayment of, the foreign capital was made in goods. The unfavorable and favorable balances in American foreign trade before the war represented merely different phases of the debtor position of the United States.

The United States was a prosperous debtor. The national income increased at a faster rate than the population. Wealth accumulated. The country was able not only to repay the money due abroad, but also to invest money of its own in foreign enterprises. The value of American foreign investments increased from a half-billion dollars in 1900 to nearly two billion dollars in 1912. Most of this was invested in Latin American countries. It may be seen, therefore, that, even before the war, the United States was on the way to becoming a creditor nation. This change was greatly accelerated, however by the war and postwar conditions. Not only did the government of the United States lend the Allies large sums for war purposes, but after the war much larger sums were lent on private account to finance Europe's reconstruction. By 1930, America's investments abroad, aside from war loans, totaled more than fifteen billion dollars, nearly a third of which was invested in Europe. America's postwar creditor position has been accompanied by a favorable trade balance, the loans being used for the purchase of American goods, but since the depression virtually put a stop to American foreign lending, it may be presumed that the United States is entering into the second state, or unfavorable-trade-balance stage, of a creditor country, when imports exceed exports.

THE FOREIGN TRADE POLICY OF THE UNITED STATES

America's postwar foreign trade policy was not consistent with its creditor position. During the postwar period the government undertook an intensive program of export trade promotion, made possible by loans to foreign countries, but obstructed the final payment for its increased exports by raising the tariff against imports. The depression, however, has developed a fuller appreciation of the double-entry relationships in international trade and has brought about a revision of our foreign trade policy, which now takes into account the fact that imports constitute the principal means of payment for sums due us from foreign sales and loans.

THE IMPASSE IN WORLD TRADE

The inconsistency in our postwar foreign trade policy was in a large measure an outgrowth of dislocations in international economic relations following the World War. The war resulted in a redirection of economic activities throughout the world. The adversaries tried to become independent of one another. They gave up their export trade and bent their efforts to fighting and to manufacturing war materials. They became increasingly dependent upon other countries for foodstuffs and raw materials. In response to the war demands of the belligerents and to the nominal economic demands of those countries formerly supplied by the warring countries in Europe, the productive systems of North and South America, Japan, and Australia were greatly expanded. The demands of postwar reconstruction supported by foreign loans maintained the high level of production in the non-European countries even after the war. The expansion of industry in the non-European countries did not proceed, however, along normal lines of economic development. Their newly developed production facilities in great part replaced, rather than supplemented, those of Europe. When, therefore, Europe later more fully resumed its economic activities, serious maladjustments occurred in international trade. Europe became increasingly able to supply its own markets and was successful in regaining a part of the foreign markets that it had lost through the war. Europe found it necessary, moreover, to stimulate its export trade in order to obtain the foreign exchange required to service and repay loans obtained from abroad. Thus not only were the former markets of newly expanded industries in the non-European countries diminished, but also the domestic markets of those countries were threatened by a flood of competitive foreign goods. The European countries raised their import barriers to protect their reconstructed industries and to reduce demands for foreign exchange for commercial accounts in order to facilitate their debt payments. The non-European countries also raised their import barriers to protect at least in the domestic market their overexpanded industries from foreign competition. This action further reduced the foreign exchange available to the European countries for debt payments to, and purchases of goods from, the non-European countries and greatly intensified the international problems of trade and finance and contributed in some measure to the collapse of international economic relations in the depression period.

The problem confronting the United States now is the rehabilitation of international commerce not only for the sake of economic recovery in the United States, but also for the peace and prosperity of the world, without which permanent domestic recovery is doubtful.

THE RELATION OF THE UNITED STATES
TO WORLD ECONOMY

Although economic isolation is perhaps possible for the United States to a greater degree than to any other country, the maintenance of this country's present high level of production and a fuller realization of its economic potentialities lie in the development of closer international commercial relationships. The United States is the world's largest producer of cotton, corn, wheat, tobacco, hogs, coal, petroleum, pig iron, copper, lead, zinc, and other raw materials. It produces 80 per cent of the world's automobiles. It is the second largest producer of cattle and wool. It is the most important producer of locomotives and railway equipment. And since the war it has become the leading producer of chemicals and machinery. Not only does it normally produce a surplus for sale abroad of most of the raw materials named above, but also its large-scale production operations in its most important manufacturing industries are geared to the foreign demand. It is the world's leading exporting country. Moreover, the United States is the world's largest consumer of sugar, coffee, silk, tin, and rubber. Its imports, consisting in large part of raw materials for manufacturing, are needed to complement and supplement domestic supplies. The amount of its import trade is second only to that of the United Kingdom. The United States has become a great power in world economy because it has been able to take advantage of the factors favoring large-scale production methods.

Operating in large part under conditions of increasing returns, American economy has been able to maintain the highest living standards in the world. American wages as well as the American per capita income are higher than those of other countries. Owing to the greater use of machinery and electrical power and the greater capital investment in factories and equipment, the productivity of the workers of the United States exceeds that of the workers of any other country. The ability of American industry to reduce costs and increase wages, at first made possible by a vast domestic market, is to a growing degree dependent upon foreign markets. If we are to continue to enjoy the benefits of a large-scale production economy for which we possess special advantages, if we are to realize our economic potentialities, we must seek to rehabilitate, maintain, and develop world trade.

Because of its economic power, its leading share in world trade, its vast potential markets for foreign goods, and its large supplies of raw materials and manufactures for foreign countries, the United States may, if it will, exert a tremendous influence in the economic affairs of the world. In view of that fact, and inasmuch as its postwar foreign trade policy contributed in a measure to the building of barriers to international trade and the present world trend toward economic nationalism, the United States has a responsibility which it cannot shirk. The future of world trade is in large measure in its hands. The question which it must help to decide is whether the world is to be broken up into warring nationalistic economic units or whether it will become a more peaceful and more closely united economy. In order to appreciate this responsibility of the United States toward the future of world trade, it is necessary to analyze the problem of economic nationalism which threatens the economic progress and peace of the world.

THE PROBLEM OF ECONOMIC NATIONALISM IN INTERNATIONAL RELATIONS

The increase in and the new forms of restrictions on imports which have been so prevalent since the depression, although indirectly related to the rise of economic protectionism in that such protectionism helped to produce the depression, did not in the beginning grow out of a deliberate plan by various nations to become economically self-sufficient; they resulted from a desperate effort on the part of certain countries to protect their currencies in the midst of chaos in international trade and finance by eliminating or reducing their unfavorable trade balances. The aim was an expansion of exports as well as a restriction of imports. Governments were not able to withstand for long, however, the pressure from politically entrenched economic interests to use these restrictive import measures for the purpose of providing those interests with increased protection. Moreover, when the efforts at trade balancing became widespread, when it became evident that an expansion of exports was not possible in the face of worldwide restrictions on imports, and when, therefore, it became clear that countries would soon have to make a choice between economic nationalism on the one hand, and international trade on the other, as a basis for the formulation of economic policy, the protectionist interests lost no opportunity to influence that choice by spreading the specious propaganda of economic nationalism.

ECONOMIC POLICIES PRIOR TO ECONOMIC NATIONALISM

The objective of economic policies, whether mercantilism, physiocracy, free trade, or protectionism, but with the possible exception of economic nationalism, has been, until recently, the assurance of plenty. The differences in the policies which have been pursued with a view to obtaining such an assurance are accounted for in large part by the difference in the technological, economic, and political factors which have prevailed at different times. Although economic nationalism is relatively a recent phenomenon, being the logical outcome of the growth of insatiable protectionism since the latter part of the nineteenth century, governmental regulation and restriction of foreign trade has long been a part of these various policies. Explanatory illustrations of this may readily be given. For example:

(1) In early times, before the rise of our modern pecuniary economy, when self-sufficiency was a fact rather than an aim, and when economic well-being was regarded as dependent upon a plentiful supply of consumption goods, exports were restricted whereas imports were encouraged.

(2) Then, in the era of mercantilism, when the area of the market was expanding, when participation in that expansion depended upon military power, and when military power was in turn dependent in great measure upon liquid financial resources, restrictions were imposed upon imports with a view to maintaining a favorable balance of trade in order, first, to obtain a plentiful supply of precious metals, and second, for the purpose of punishing, and diminishing the power of, foreign countries.

Certain differences between the protectionism of mercantilism and modern protectionism are: (*a*) the former was desired because of its inflationary effects whereas the latter is desired to offset effects of inflation; (*b*) the former was an outgrowth of aggressive action against old forces whereas the latter is a defense against new forces.

(3) Later, the free trade era developed. Owing to its need for larger markets, lower costs of raw materials and of foodstuffs, and owing, also, to the necessity of accepting in an agricultural world agricultural imports in payment for industrial exports in order to take full advantage of its industrial supremacy growing out of the Industrial Revolution, England espoused the cause of free trade and sought by means of recip-

rocal trade agreements to reduce the barriers to international trade.

(4) The free trade era was, however, short-lived; the trend in tariffs since that time has been steadily upward.

The reaction to free trade may be explained with reference to the following considerations:

(*a*) Competition of cheap agricultural products from the United States made possible by the development of inland transportation and the application of machine methods to agriculture. This instance of agricultural protectionism, which would not be justified on the basis of List's arguments for protectionism, is an early indication of the tendency in recent times to adapt government regulation of foreign trade in order to protect existing economic interests against destructive competition resulting from new technological and economic forces.

(*b*) The decline in importance of independent merchants and the rise of the industrialists.

(*c*) The realization, perhaps, that the attainment of power and prestige under free trade is dependent upon naval supremacy.

(*d*) The realization that military strength is dependent to a degree upon industrialization.

(*e*) The desire of newly formed nations to preserve their political independence; for example, Germany and Italy.

(5) The trend toward economic self-sufficiency has been especially marked since the World War and is reflected in the decline in American exports, especially in those of agricultural products.

THE ISSUE INVOLVED

Recent developments in technology have made possible a standard of living and an accumulation of wealth hardly dreamed of in the nineteenth century. They have brought modern society within sight of the goal of economic plenty which was the objective of economic policies pursued in the past. The failure, however, to adjust economic and political institutions to these developments, greatly accelerated by the World War, has not only prevented the full enjoyment of the benefits of those developments, but has resulted in periodical collapses of the present economy, accentuated by postwar difficulties, and interjecting into economic life an intolerable degree of uncertainty.

The objective, therefore, of present-day economic policies is primarily not economic plenty, but economic security without which the enjoyment of plenty is not possible. The trend of government policies is, accordingly, toward economic planning. In the United States such planning had already been preceded by efforts among the various economic classes to achieve some degree of stability. This was reflected in associations and economic institutions of various sorts and by government regulation of public utilities, trade competition, and banking, culminating in the New Deal programs. The issue now is, however, whether that planning shall proceed on the basis of economic nationalism under pressure from economic interests, now well entrenched, who would freeze the *status quo,* limit our technological and economic possibilities, and establish a permanent economic hierarchy of the various class elements in present society in order to retain their favorable position, or whether it shall proceed on the basis of a world economy, making available to mankind the full benefits of natural advantages in production, and making possible further advancements in technology in order that all human beings may enjoy a more abundant life. In order to appreciate fully the problems involved in this issue, it is necessary to analyze the economic instability for which economic nationalism is offered as a remedy.

THE DESIRE FOR ECONOMIC SECURITY

Although the great development in technology which began with the Industrial Revolution and has continued ever since at an accelerated rate accounts in great measure for the high degree of specialization in production and for the economic interdependency among nations which has made possible the relatively high standards of living of today, it is, nevertheless, because of the maladjustments that it has produced in an uncontrolled, competitive economy, a force making for instability in our economic life. The increase of speed and carrying capacity in, and the consequent lower costs of, inland and ocean transportation have resulted in greatly expanded markets. This has so greatly increased the opportunities for specialization that, with the mechanization of industry and the application of motor power to machinery, standardized mass production has become in general characteristic of modern industry. However, the mechanization of mass production industries imposes on such industries a huge burden of overhead costs. This burden exerts a pressure to increase production to capacity and for the carrying of this capacity production a steady market is required. Thus specialization entailing larger overhead costs makes for an economy much more sensitive to market fluctuations, and accentuates the intensity and magnitude of economic depressions.

At the same time, the greater use of machinery tends to displace labor and consequently reduces purchasing power upon which the market is dependent. Whereas the inventions of the nineteenth century, such as those in transportation, created new needs and resulted therefore in an expansion of the production system, many of the technical advances of today result in labor-saving devices and unemployment.

Economic maladjustments have been greatly aggravated by the World War. The war quickened the tempo of technical progress and increased the capacity of production in agriculture and industry in non-European countries. Owing to the inelasticity of demand for agricultural products, agriculture experienced the depressing effects of overproduction sooner than other industries. The war, moreover, left Europe with a huge debt burden for which the non-European creditor countries, faced with problems of overproduction, refused to take goods in payment. Out of these complications in international trade and finance, which, through excessive inflation, resulted, in many countries, in a sudden redistribution of the national income, grew the currency depreciation that finally and entirely destroyed the prewar feeling of economic security.

Although technological improvements in the United States make possible the production of more goods for consumption, its competitive system, seemingly, is not adequate, without an increasing degree of intelligent regulation and control, for the distribution of the increased output to the consumers. It may be observed that economic depressions are greater in magnitude and duration in the most highly industrialized countries, because the demand for durable goods is more elastic than that for perishable consumers' goods. Thus it may be seen that economic stability, which is essential to the economic security of all classes in a modern economy, demands a protection similar to that given to investments in industry. Owing to the lack of adequate regulation of competition, an effort to eliminate competition in order to protect such investment is evidenced in the trend toward combination and monopoly. And, inasmuch as labor competes with the investment class for the product of industry, and the farmer competes with the manufacturer for his share in the national income, this trend toward combination and monopoly is found in the fields of labor and agriculture, as well as in other fields.

This conflict among powerful economic groups is not confined to the sphere of economics but is carried over into the sphere of politics, each group seeking to determine governmental policies for the protection and advancement of its interests. Economic legislation such as tariff making or the fixing of minimum wages or hours of labor, enacted in favor of one group, disturbs the existing economic relations in society as a whole, and adversely affects the economic opportunities of other groups, which in turn exert their political strength to obtain compensating benefits. The result is that government, in order to fulfill its function of maintaining equilibrium in the economic structure, becomes increasingly involved in the affairs of private enterprise, irrespective of what the traditional practices or policies of the administration in power might be. In the early days of rugged individualism, when private enterprise was well able to take care of its interests without government attention, the United States adhered to the philosophy of *laissez faire* and deprecated government regulation as a step in the direction of socialism. But now that the economic problems of our society are growing in magnitude and private enterprise is less able to cope with them, many sections of business and agricultural opinion favor to a greater or lesser degree a planned economy and look upon government regulation and control as a means by which vested interests may be protected. Because the government is sometimes unable or disinclined to use direct measures to control production or prices, the tariff and other trade restrictions have become outstanding in importance as measures for obtaining protection and privilege.

Thus, government regulation and control of the economic activities of the nation is no longer an issue, but a fact. The present issue, however, need not necessarily be that of Fascism or Communism, each with its own program of economic nationalism; that is, it need not be a question of economic planning in the interest of one or the other of extremely opposed groups in a national economy. A sane solution may lie in a middle course in which the interests of all groups will receive a reasonable amount of protection, but in which economic planning will proceed upon the basis of a world economy, making possible to society the great benefits of international trade and developments in technology and increased wealth and income resulting therefrom.

THE FACTOR OF NATIONALISM

It is well to recognize at this point that, besides the desire for economic security, the rise of political nationalism, which has been particularly strong as a result of the World War, is another force bearing upon the trend toward economic isolation, to the prospect of which certain economic and technological factors may lend an appeal. The growth of nationalistic sentiment has been reflected in the political unification of Germany and Italy in the latter part of the nineteenth century, the political separations within the British empire, the formation of new countries after the war, and, recently, the political solidarity achieved under the Fascist and Nazi régimes. With the growth of international economic dependency, nations have become increasingly vulnerable with respect to economic weapons which have acquired a new importance in military strategy. The economic penetration of powerful countries into the backward areas has created conditions which are especially favorable to the rise of nationalism in those areas. This fact, especially in view of the political antagonisms resulting from the war, accounts in large measure for the effort that countries are making to establish their political independence upon an economic basis. Even the United Kingdom, long the chief exponent of a free trade doctrine, has taken steps in that direction, realizing as a lesson of the war that whereas naval supremacy may starve the enemy, it does not necessarily assure to the naval power supplies of food and raw materials. The withdrawal of the United States from European affairs after the war and the growing disillusionment over the ability of the League of Nations to assure political stability have increased the feeling of political insecurity and of the need for self-defense and, consequently, economic self-sufficiency. Although national self-sufficiency would mean a lower standard of living than would otherwise be possible, many people as a result of the postwar inflation and the recent depression have already adjusted themselves to a lower scale of living. In wealthier countries, manufactured and primary products are less important in the domestic economy relative to houses, personal services, and similar factors which are less directly involved in international trade. Diversification as a solution to the problem of economic instability has already been carried appreciably far in agriculture, and recent achievements in the field of technology would seem to make national self-sufficiency possible in some degree.

THE FALLACIES OF ECONOMIC NATIONALISM

Before considering the possibilities of a greater degree of economic planning upon a world-economy basis, a brief examination should be made of the pretensions of economic nationalism as a solution to the problems of economic and political instability. "Planning for [economic] stabilization on an exclusive national basis is analogous to the attempt of separate industries to stabilize their own prices and control their own output. It proceeds by a series of restrictions....

the net effect of which is to raise costs and prices, decrease the volume of activity and output and thus diminish real incomes all round.... It represents merely the transference of competition from smaller units to large national aggregates."[2] Thus, while competition is suppressed to a degree within the nation, it is exalted to a national basis so far as international commercial relations are involved.

Bilateralism in international trade, which is already far advanced in Europe, is one of the worst features of commercial competition on a national basis and is one of the greatest obstacles to the recovery of American foreign trade. Bilateralism, which consists in the balancing of imports and exports between one country and another, is an outgrowth of an effort by countries to obtain preferential advantages in the markets of other countries, with which they have so-called unfavorable trade balances. It results in discrimination against the trade of third countries and produces political antagonisms. International trade even under high protectionism may still be of great benefit if conducted, within the limits permitted, upon a nondiscriminatory basis and in accordance with the principle of comparative advantage, but bilateralism, in precluding multilateral trade, violates that principle and tends to nullify the benefit of international commerce, and to impose upon the economy of the countries forced to submit to it the additional burden of higher costs for raw materials and foodstuffs, which have the effect finally of eliminating these unfortunate countries from competition in world markets.

---

[2] *The Encyclopedia of the Social Sciences,* Vol. XIV, p. 314.

The struggle on a national basis for markets and raw materials, the need for which cannot be eliminated even in the most highly developed régime of national self-sufficiency, results in economic imperialism on an unprecedented scale accompanied by wars of conquest, which would make possible neither economic nor political stability. The recent military events in Manchuria and Ethiopia are illustrations of this. The countries most in need of political protection, namely, the smaller countries, would be the ones left most defenseless. Because they are more limited in their economic resources, they are especially dependent upon foreign trade and less able to achieve national self-sufficiency upon the scale which is possible to larger and more powerful countries. They are, moreover, less able to resist the pressure of bilateralism, and finally degenerate into economic, if not political, dependencies.

Planning under economic nationalism is fundamentally irrational. It encourages production under the most unfavorable conditions and stimulates the output of goods which are superfluous in view of the available supplies abroad. In the midst of plenty, it seeks to create scarcity. It seeks to insure political stability by economic preparation for war. If it is able to achieve in some slight measure its chief economic objective, the protection of investment, in connection with which the satisfaction of human wants is utterly disregarded, it is able to do so only by the suppression of social groups having other economic interests and by reducing the standards of living to a low scale. All that economic nationalism can offer us is poverty and war.

FACTORS MAKING FOR A MORE CLOSELY UNITED
WORLD ECONOMY

A sane and rational solution to our problems of economic and political instability does not lie in the economic nationalism of either Fascism or Communism, but in the adaptation of our present social institutions to our economic possibilities. We need a program which will provide a reasonable amount of protection of both investment and employment with a view to increasing the means of satisfying human wants; that is, planning for abundance. Such planning will necessarily take full advantage of the benefits of international trade and seek to promote peace by suppressing that preferential treatment in international commerce which results in political antagonisms. In other words, in order to insure both stability and plenty, it will seek to use and control by government regulation and international coöperation existing technological, economic, and political forces tending to bring national systems into closer world relationships. It has been pointed out above that the forces in the United States that are influencing the trend toward national isolation are reactionary ones, resulting from our failure to adapt our economic and political institutions to the forces evolving a world economy. The latter are essentially the fundamental and driving forces in modern civilization, and although their operation may be retarded by the friction of an imperfect social mechanism, they cannot be suppressed so long as our civilization obtains. Preëminent are the existence of comparative advantages in production, and the pressure of foreign investment.

(1) Competition in a pecuniary society is analogous to the force of gravity in physics. It exerts a pull on prices, tending to draw them together or reduce them to a common level. Comparative advantage in production which gives rise to differences in costs operates in the opposite direction, creating price differentials. Trade is the resulting process which tends to bring prices and costs into equilibrium. Although science and invention may make physically possible in a certain country the synthetic manufacture, or the replacement by substitutes, of products for which it lacks the natural resources to produce, science and invention cannot eliminate, but can only change in nature, comparative advantage and cost differences. In reducing cost differentials with respect to one product, they increase such differentials with respect to others. Even should raw materials be equally distributed among the nations of the world, comparative advantage would still operate to produce differences in costs of production in various countries, for comparative advantages arise from differences in various areas in the proportions in which the several factors of production are supplied, in human aptitudes, in industrial technique, in the distances between production centers and markets, and in numerous other factors. It may be observed that the largest volume of world trade does not move between countries in different latitudes, between which there is the greatest difference in the distribution of natural resources, but between the industrial countries of the north temperate zone. The countries which export the most machinery are those which import the most. Inasmuch as national self-sufficiency increases international cost differentials,

it is working against the forces of trade, which, being dammed by import restrictions, accumulate power and sooner or later break over the barriers. It may be doubtful, therefore, on this count alone whether any great degree of national self-sufficiency is possible. In fact, since the industrial development necessary for national self-sufficiency in most countries is dependent upon foreign supplies of raw materials, heavy machinery, and capital funds, it would appear that the growth of national self-sufficiency to the limited extent that this is possible, is basically dependent upon international trade. Notwithstanding the increased restrictions on trade following the war, American exports of machinery increased.

(2) The great developments which have occurred in transportation, on the one hand, have not only enhanced or made possible the use of natural advantages in certain regions,—for example, those for grain production and cattle and sheep raising in the western United States,—but they have also created new needs and greatly expanded the area of the market. On the other hand, the expansion of the market area has increased the possibilities of specialization in production and international economic dependency. Even the rise of nationalism has in a measure aided this development by creating larger free-trade areas. In addition to making possible a more closely integrated world economy, the advancements made in transportation as well as communication have resulted in a greater diffusion of national cultures, ideas, and scientific knowledge, providing a basis for better understanding among nations.

(3) The great benefits resulting from modern develop-

ments in technology and the expansion of world trade have been reflected in the accumulation in the industrial countries of wealth for foreign investment, which has not only in turn aided in the expansion of world markets but has also created in the world a greater community of economic interest.

This trend toward increased economic dependency among nations has been reflected in great efforts at international coöperation, of which the outstanding example consists of the economic and financial work of the League of Nations. The Montevideo Conference is an instance of an international program for promoting closer trade relations between countries having in common certain economic interests. The world wheat conference and the recent European lumber agreements are instances of economic planning on an international scale. The various international arrangements which have been or are being made with respect to the control of trade in raw materials such as nitrate, potash, mercury, copper, and sugar are evidence that economic enterprise extends beyond national boundaries and beyond the reach of national control.

THE SIGNIFICANCE TO WORLD TRADE OF THE TRADE
AGREEMENTS PROGRAM OF THE UNITED STATES

The trade agreements program of the United States government is a recognition of the fact that the problems confronting our agriculture and industry are world-wide and that they cannot be solved by domestic programs alone, but that an attempt must be made in conjunction with foreign countries whose commercial policies directly affect our own to extend some degree of economic planning to the field of international trade. The United States is taking the lead in this direction. The trade agreements program has two main objectives: one is the reciprocal reduction of the barriers to the trade between this country and foreign countries, and the other is the assurance of nondiscriminatory, or most-favored-nation, treatment of that trade. Reductions in import duties are made in accordance with the characteristics and needs of domestic industries. They are extended not only to the countries in the specific trade agreements,—these countries being for the most part the principal suppliers of the commodities named in the agreements,—but they are also generalized to all countries which do not discriminate against the commerce of the United States. Some of the commodities on which the duties are reduced are commodities which are not available in this country in sufficient quantities or which cannot be produced in this country at all on a satisfactory cost basis. On others, duty reductions are made because they represent imports which do not compete in any great degree with domestic products, either because of differences in quality or price, or because their sale is limited to certain areas. Also, reductions are made in the duties on commodities the increased imports of which will not be so large as seriously to depress the prices of like or similar domestic products. The reductions of duty on some of these—as, for example, provided for in our trade agreement with Canada with respect to lumber, cattle, and cream—are limited to a specified quantity of imports, an excess of the quantity being subject to the higher rate. Also, a duty reduction may be limited to the "off season" in the domestic marketing of the commodity affected. The reductions are moderate and are made only after an exhaustive study of all the factors involved in order to avoid any possible sudden shock to industry and to permit of any adjustments which may be necessary.

The increase in imports permitted by judicious reductions in our tariff result in a larger supply of dollar exchange abroad upon which the larger purchases of American exports are dependent and by means of which the concessions obtained from foreign countries on American products may be taken advantage of. The products on which concessions are obtained from a foreign country with which a trade agreement is entered into are for the most part products of which the United States is the major or an important foreign supplier to that country. Our trade agreements provide not only for unconditional most-favored-nation treatment of our commerce with the countries concerned with respect to import duties and customs administration, but also for fair and equitable treatment of our commerce with respect to exchange control and import quotas and other forms of quantitative restrictions on trade. The assurance of nondiscriminatory treatment of our commerce abroad is necessary not only to prevent the concessions obtained for American exports from being nullified by more favorable concessions to third countries, but also to protect our commerce in general from the practices of bilateralism.

Announcements of intention to negotiate trade agreements have been made with respect to eighteen countries, which in 1929 accounted for 41 per cent of our imports and 42 per cent of our exports. In 1934, the percentages were 45.5 per cent and 39 per cent, respectively. Thus far, agreements have been concluded with fourteen of those countries; namely, Belgium, Brazil, Canada, Colombia, Cuba, Haiti, Honduras, the Netherlands, Sweden, Switzerland, France, Finland, Nicaragua, and Guatemala. Other countries will be added to this list as the program proceeds.

By means of its trade agreements program, the United States is accomplishing much toward rehabilitating international trade on a sane and rational basis. It is helping to restore trade to its normal channels and to increase its opportunities as well as those of other countries in the world markets. In exerting a liberalizing force in world commerce, it is helping to relieve the economic pressure which is forcing many other countries into bilateralism and political aggression.

THE FUTURE OF COMMERCE IN WORLD TRADE

Realizing that its economic frontiers extend beyond its political boundaries, that the future of its economic development lies in the expansion of its foreign markets, and that its material well-being is held in common with that of other nations, the United States will continue to work in the interests of world trade. Its purpose in entering into agreements with foreign countries regarding trade matters will be to increase the benefits of trade, not only for itself, but also for other countries, for only to the extent that all countries benefit will world commerce grow and prosper. It will therefore continue to stand for equal opportunities in the world markets for all nations, and to seek reductions in the barriers to international commerce. So far as the pursuance of this policy is successful, the people of this nation as well as those of foreign nations will enjoy a more abundant life and greater economic and political security. And the United States will be regarded more and more as a force in international relations for peace and prosperity.

MILITARY POLICY AND NATIONAL SECURITY

———

DAVID P. BARROWS

PROFESSOR OF POLITICAL SCIENCE
IN THE UNIVERSITY OF CALIFORNIA

Lecture delivered October 21, 1936

MILITARY POLICY AND NATIONAL SECURITY

THERE IS A COMMON VIEW that national security—and this may mean complete immunity from foreign invasion or disturbance—completely fulfills the objective of modern states. But it should be clear that this objective does not cover the whole intent and purpose of all states at the present time. They are not satisfied with what they are or have. They want to be greater and have more. This has always been so, and it is not less so now than formerly. The first duty of a state is to defend and protect its own, but very rarely does a people conceive this to be its sole mission. National security is a part of national policy, but not the whole. Extraordinary efforts have been made in recent years to induce all states to rest as they are, to perpetuate and sanctify the *status quo*. These efforts may satisfy the objectives of some states, but not of all. Hence, it seems impossible to unite all states of the world to give collective defense to the political map of the world as it now stands. And even if it were, the passage of years would modify the general situation so that the *status quo* with its collective security would seem to certain states oppressive and unbearable.

It should also be clear that the term "national security" may be used to cloak designs that extend beyond national security. The phrase is overworked; it is accepted for what it is not. To assume that national security is the sole objective of modern nations and the sole reason for their display of military preparations is to believe that a mask is a true face.

War was defined a hundred years ago by the famous German soldier and military authority, General Karl von Clausewitz, as a continuation of politics or policy by means of violence.[1] There is no combating this definition. Either war is purposeless, or it is the effort of a state to obtain its objectives by warlike means when pacific means have failed. War would be completely senseless if it were not directed to achieving the success of a policy that cannot be obtained except by the sword. It was Clausewitz's definition of war, his discernment that war was an instrument of policy, which inspired the Kellogg-Briand Pact.

The mistake of the upholders of the Pact was in supposing that all modern nations would, with equal sincerity, pledge themselves to such renunciation. It should be evident already that not all will do so. And this is so because there is no one policy which is common to all modern states. Each has its own. Some of them have policies which cannot be put into effect except through war. And recent events have shown that some nations have purposes so definite and hardened

---

[1] The voluminous writings of Clausewitz were edited, after his death in 1831, by his wife, Marie von Clausewitz. They amount to ten volumes under the original title of *Hinterlassene Werke über Krieg und Kriegführung.* The first three volumes contain his treatise on the philosophy of war, *Vom Kriege;* the remaining volumes deal with the history of the campaigns of Napoleon, whose conduct of war Clausewitz labored to analyze and describe. The philosophic dissertation, "On War," is the masterpiece, the basis of military studies for the past century. In Germany, it has been printed many times, the thirteenth or fourteenth edition appearing three years ago. But owing to its posthumous appearance, to the incompleted character of part of it, and possibly to faulty arrangement, present-day scholarship in Germany is still unsatisfied with the form of the work and is occupied with producing a "definitive" edition. *Vom Kriege* was translated into English in 1873 by the British officer, Colonel J. J. Graham, and has appeared in more than one printing.

that they will become violators of the Kellogg-Briand Pact rather than renounce war to secure them. The result of this is that, among the signers of such a pact, those with a genuine will to renunciation of war find their position weakened; for those nations which perhaps do not intend to keep their obligation occupy with respect to war a position of advantage, the advantage that they have not suppressed "the will to war" and can act more promptly, resolutely, and effectively than the nations which hope and believe they have cast warfare into the discard.

Among the sixty-odd recognized states of the modern world, there are numerous nations, and they are not the least cultivated and admirable, which could be counted upon, under any circumstance which we can foresee, to renounce war and all its preparations. These nations are devoid of aggressive ambitions. Most of them, moreover, are so small—and this operates to the disadvantage of their influence—that modern warfare would be their ruin. Any armaments they might create would be insufficient in the face of danger, and might even increase that danger. These nations make a moral appeal which is by no means wholly ineffective, but they must guard their neutrality, avoid responsibility, and, in a way, "walk quietly all their days." The greater nations, on the whole, will not adopt this attitude. Hence, sincere efforts to bring the greater nations to peace through a renunciation of warfare have failed.

Of the half-dozen major states in the world which rank as Great Powers, there is obvious disagreement in respect to policies and intentions. The British people, and the American people with them, seem thoroughly convinced of the wrong, the waste, the cost to civilization, of warfare. But the English people have a world-wide empire to defend, and doubtless they would fight to preserve it, for it is indispensable to their welfare, although England would obviously prefer a collective security for this empire. The preference seems manifest from the efforts of the British government to stay the hand of Italy against Ethiopia. In fact, some recent British writers have frankly stated that Great Britain is no longer competent alone to defend the empire, and that its security must rest upon a collective security.

The people of the United States are in the most secure position of any in the world. It is hard for them to visualize danger as other peoples feel danger. Nevertheless, they are probably still convinced that their national security rests upon the security of the entire Western Hemisphere from any further domination or aggression on the part of the Old World. And while this people can no longer be counted upon to use force, or the threat of force, to maintain the John Hay policy in the Far East, they probably would go to war to defend their interpretation of the doctrine that originated with President Monroe.

The French Republic has, since the World War, given every evidence of anxiety lest there be fresh attack from Germany. To avoid this, France secured the demilitarization of the Rhineland, the disarmament of its main opponent, the organization of the Little Entente, and, above all, pledges of armed support by other nations in the event of future invasion. The French Republic, moreover, has given to its eastern frontier a maze of intricate underground defenses, the Maginot line, that has no parallel among works of fortification.

French security would seem to rest most securely upon a strict policy of defense. But French diplomacy has recently reversed this policy by contracting an alliance with Soviet Russia that will compel France to go to the assistance of Russia if that nation is simultaneously attacked by two other powers. This treaty, in other words, would commit France to an offensive against Germany if Germany, and some other state, should become involved in a war with Russia. The alliance changes the French position from one of strong defense to one of pledged offensive in certain contingencies. The response to this was immediate and dramatic. National Socialist Germany immediately occupied the Rhineland and the bridgeheads west of the Rhine. Belgium renounced its alliance with France as no longer a safe relationship, for so small a nation, with a nation that has accepted responsibility for aggressive war.

The other great states include Russia, Italy, Germany, and Japan. None of these states can be trusted further to preserve its renunciation of war. The first of them, while it possesses an amplitude of territory and richness of resources, is a state of militant revolution. It is a crusader for the world realization of proletarian Communism. The Red army has a double mission: to defend Communism within the territory of the Soviet state, and to aid proletarian attack upon capitalist society under foreign states as well. This tactic, which was unanimously and enthusiastically approved as recently as the Seventh World Congress of the Third International at Moscow fifteen months ago, makes impossible a covenant with Soviet Russia, renouncing war. Italy and Japan plead the necessity of augmenting national territory to gain space and livelihood for increasing populations. Germany is undoubtedly resolved to regain its position as the foremost land military power and to free itself from every vestige of the servitudes imposed by the Treaty of Versailles.

Eighteen years have elapsed since the cessation of the World War, and considering the theorem that a nation is not tempted to wage war more than once in a generation, or three times in a century, the war psychology that distinguishes several of these nations is reason for surprise. But the postwar generation in these nations has matured rapidly. It has been artificially incited by militaristic propaganda. It has been given a training in the hardships and severity of warfare that would hardly be tolerable if the menace of war were not believed in.

In the resulting danger, England has stood actively for the principle of collective security, for the support of the League of Nations, and for making its authority effective to prevent coercion and violence by one nation against another. But obviously the achievement is beyond the present capacity of statesmanship, which finds itself confronted by a nationalism too intense to yield obedience to a league.

The League of Nations might have been more successful if its membership had been restricted instead of world-wide. The attempt to exert the authority of the League everywhere seems premature. As a European mechanism, unhampered by the participation of non-European countries, the League of Nations still might be a strong force. Obviously, coöperation and sacrifice to meet European difficulties cannot be expected from non-European states whose interests are not engaged, in whom no sense of responsibility exists, and whose contribution in any event, whether intellectual or material, would be negligible.

Possessing unrivaled material resources and potential military power which were decisive in 1918, and which might be decisive again, the United States has definitely refused membership and responsibility in the League of Nations, and refuses to regard any war anywhere as necessarily America's war. In fact, the rôle of the United States in the support of peaceful and coöperative relations would not seem to be a European rôle. The United States has its particular sphere of responsibility, and that is for the Western Hemisphere, for the security of the states of the New World. In this field the United States has been neither neglectful nor unsuccessful. That expectancy of attack, that sense of hazard to national existence that prevails in Europe, does not haunt the political life of the two Americas. Diplomacy has recorded triumphs not yet attainable in Europe. Boundary disputes, with a few minor exceptions, have been settled, and settled by concession, by negotiation, and by arbitration. Adherence to principles of international law is stronger in the New World than in the Old. The recent furious struggle between Bolivia and Paraguay over the Chaco Boreal should not blind us to the superior and advantageous international situation in the two Americas. The rôle of the United States is less in coöperation with European states to preserve the latters' fortunes and solve their rivalries than it is to prevent those rivalries from gaining fresh lodgment in the Western Hemisphere. The United States has virtually assumed the protection on the sea of the two American continents, and its traditional doctrine opposes both warfare and coercion applied by a non-American state to an American state. That such coercion is not discernible today is nothing less than an extraordinary triumph for the foreign policy developed by the early statesmen of this Republic.

While the success of the United States in its policy with respect to the Western Hemisphere may be judged well-nigh complete, the government has nevertheless made two sacrifices in recent years of policies for which it had long contended. The first has to do with China and the Far Eastern field of controversy. Under the statesmanship of the early part of this century, the United States sought to preserve the integrity of China against partition or the creation of spheres of influence. This was accomplished by the annunciation of the doctrine of the Open Door, adhesion to which by all interested states was accomplished by John Hay. In a lasting adherence to this policy, the United States now appears to have failed. The policy may still be regarded by our government and people as right, equitable, and of general economic advantage, but not sufficiently vital to justify a commitment to war.

It seems equally clear that the long contest waged by the United States government for recognition of the American theory of the freedom of the seas—a theory which was a factor in our war with Great Britain in 1812–14—has also been dropped as a fundamental which we will defend. The support of this doctrine reached its culmination and its most dangerous point in the first two years of the World War. With any nation other than Great Britain it might well have resulted in war. Its defiance by Germany put the United States into the war. Recently, by action of both the President and Congress, the government has retired from the extreme advocacy of the rights of neutral states in warfare, including the right of continuous trade with belligerent nations under a neutral flag. Perhaps we could do no less, not merely as a means of avoidance of war but also of showing due consideration and respect for the authority of the League of Nations. At any rate, it may be supposed that, if a European nation is recalcitrant to a decision of the League of Nations, and has imposed upon it by the League an economic embargo or blockade, the United States will no longer insist, as it has in the past, that by reason of its neutral position it will send ships and cargoes under the American flag through this blockade.

What may be called military preparedness has had a very marked development since the end of the World War. It is not only that the combatant European states of 1914, or the new states which have succeeded them, have again standing or "peacetime" forces comparable to those of 1914, when Europe was described as an "armed camp," but also that these new postwar armies are capable of much greater destructive power than their precursors of 1914. Fire power has been multiplied by the general adoption of mechanized small arms, by the increased amounts and calibers of field artillery, by motorization of transport, and by the development of war aviation. If an organized and armed unit could do surprising feats of arms in 1914 or in 1918, a unit of like size and kind can do much more today.[2]

The organization of national power in war has been equally developed. The French have devised a new standard of estimating war power, *potentiel de la guerre*. This theory no longer merely counts the strength of battalions, or "man power";—this is insufficient as a standard;—it counts everything in a nation's resources that can be made useful in war, and it contemplates that nothing thus useful will be overlooked or be unready for employment.[3] The Soviet Russians have shaped their planned economy toward a war economy; their industrialization takes the form of the mass production of war materials. The location of their industrial centers is deliberately determined by remoteness from the frontiers, in order thus to gain security against attack from the air. Their propaganda agencies frankly represent to the mass of the Russian people the expectation of attack from capitalist countries for the specific purpose of overthrowing the proletarian state.

---

[2] The present armed state of the world may be studied in the League of Nations *Armaments Year Book* (Geneva), published annually since 1924. A useful manual of comparative modern armaments, with brief suggestive essays on a variety of military topics, is *Die Rüstung der Welt, eine Umschau über das Heer- und Kriegswesen der fremden Staaten,* by Lieutenant-Colonel Wilhelm Müder-Loebnitz (Berlin, 1935). With this may be used Rudolf zu der Luth, *Wehrwissenschaftlicher Atlas;* and, for naval strength, Janes's *Fighting Ships.*

[3] *Potentiel de la guerre* is discussed in recent French military literature; also in an article by General Horst von Metzsch, "War Potential," in *The Problem of Disarmament* (edited by Schmidt and Grabowsky, English supplement of *Zeitschrift für Politik,* Berlin, 1933).

Italy, too, is on a complete war footing, and not only do its resources for war seem to be organized in a manner far superior to that of 1914, but the morale of the people is controlled and the confidence of success through arms has been increased by victory in Ethiopia.

Germany is on its way back to a predominating military position in Europe, and the forces at present under arms and serving with the colors equal its standing army of 1914. All that delays its complete readiness is the development of a vast trained reserve, the accomplishment of which may be expected by 1938.

France has been recognized as the leading country to take full advantage of the military lessons of the world conflict and to adapt its organization, training, and preparation to accord with the most detailed studies of war experience.

Such is the situation of Europe today, without counting the armed condition of eastern European states, such as Poland and the successors of the Austro-Hungarian empire, wherever they are not prevented by the limitations imposed upon them as enemy belligerents in 1918. They express their sense of doubt in respect to the political future by developing to the utmost of their resources their war machinery. If Europe was an armed camp in 1914, it is a much more highly armed camp today.

The question is often raised, How far has the World War altered the historical character of warfare? This question must always be looked at from the different aspects of what is called "tactics" and what is denominated "strategy." Tactics, or the organization and conduct of soldiers in action, constantly change. Every improvement in weapons modifies the tactics whereby weapons can be effectively used. The tactics of today are entirely different from the tactics of Napoleon or of Frederick the Great or of Gustavus Adolphus or of the Roman legions, and this is primarily so because weapons alter. New weapons compel new forms of organization and new methods of engagement when battle is joined. The modifications in tactics produced by the World War and developed since the World War are, many of them, extreme departures from the tactics employed before this long and terrible testing of what men can endure and what they may accomplish on the field of battle. A large part of the mechanical ingenuity of the race, to say nothing of the efforts of the military profession, is today expended in devising new and more powerful arms, and to the discovery of proper tactics wherewith to employ these arms or to devise protection against them. The range and rapidity of scientific discovery and invention, the constant development of the engineering art, improvements in medical science: all these things contribute to the necessity of constantly devising new tactics and discarding the old.

Strategy, on the contrary, does not change fundamentally from one type of warfare to another. Strategy is the movement and concentration of forces previous to battle. Its main objective is to bring superior power to bear upon the weakest part of the enemy's resistance. The English soldier and scholar, General Sir Frederick Maurice, in a recent volume, has explored the question whether the principles of strategy have been modified by the World War. I think he judges that they have not changed.[4] These fundamentals must still guide and instruct the commander. But, although they have not altered in principle, they may alter in the form of their application. Thus, surprise, the method of the greatest commanders, has been made increasingly difficult or impossible through the development of modern systems of communication and detection, and particularly by observation from the air. It would today be impossible for a Napoleon to effect the unexpected concentration of a Grand Army on Ulm, or for a Stonewall Jackson to surprise an opponent at Chancellorsville. Prolonged rain and storm might blind opposing air forces to such a degree that tactical surprise would be possible, and in future warfare there may be no cessation, no periods of seasonal repose as in the past, no winter quarters for a wearied army; rather, perhaps, campaigns will be conducted and tactical surprise effected in the midst of storms, when snow, sleet, and rain blind enemy air observation and conceal the rapid movement of forces intent on making the surprise attack.

Nevertheless, the very difficulty of gaining by surprise in the field of combat has turned strategy to consider surprise at the opening of war: surprise, in other words, by the deliberate disregard of conventions for formalizing the commencement of war. The next war, so often discussed, will presumably be unpreceded by governmental declaration or even by rupture of diplomatic relations. It is seen as a sudden,

---

[4] *Principles of Strategy, A Study of the Application of the Principles of War*, by Major-General Sir F. Maurice, Professor of Military Studies in the University of London (New York, 1930).

unexpected attack, attack in which the entire available force of the aggressor is thrown in with the purpose of anticipating opposition, rupturing frontier defense, scattering the usual covering forces, and, with withering might suddenly applied, winning a "victory of annihilation." Wars, to achieve any national purpose worth while, must be short; and a short war, as well as a victorious war, is the justification for military preparation. There is nothing which modern military leaders are striving more to avoid than stalemate, warfare of position, the stabilized trenches, and the protraction of conflict that were characteristic in 1914–18. Unless victory can be won promptly, war wastes the victor as well as the vanquished. It becomes fruitless, and its folly is disclosed. Therefore, say its theorists, its commencement must be so rapid that it can immediately win its objectives.

Now, in conclusion, as long as nations have soldiers, it is the duty and obligation of soldiers to prepare for war. And at the present time this preparation cannot be too scientific, too thorough, or too competent. The extent to which these preparations are made depends upon many things; primarily on the degree of security of geographical position and the security that comes from prestige which victory and decisive action in war have brought, and which endures for a time; but always and fundamentally it depends upon the policies adopted by the peoples and the governments that armed forces merely serve. Again, and constantly, we must emphasize the importance of policy. If the policies of a state are aggressive, if they are directed to the liquidation of treaty restrictions, as are those of Germany; to the enlargement of territories, as are those of Italy and Japan; to the accomplishment of world revolution, as are those of Russia, armed forces are obviously developed to make these policies effective and to support them when crises or opportunities emerge. If other states, or any states like them, are in the zone of danger, they too must arm.

Between peace and warfare, there nevertheless intervenes the task of the statesman. All nations rely upon the governmental organization both to keep the peace and to preserve national interest, and government extends its efforts in what is called diplomacy. Here is the field where peace may be preserved, but both governments and peoples must be schooled not merely to a spirit of understanding and friendliness but also to a willingness to make concessions.

In the inevitable collision of national interests, when the belligerent spirit rises to the danger point and governments strive with one another for advantage, there come times when a nation must either fight or change its mind. It is at this point that concessions must be made, if conflict is to be avoided. It is the responsibility of statesmanship to discover the equitable mean between the exaggerated claims of the participants and to propose a solution. It has not often been the practice of the stronger rival to search for and propose these adjustments, but in the nature of the present organization of political society, the greater concessions must frequently be offered by the greater nations. And the maxim of Burke must be continually borne in mind, that "the greater power may offer concession with honor."

THE POLICY OF THE UNITED STATES IN THE PACIFIC AND THE FAR EAST

CHESTER H. ROWELL
EDITOR OF THE SAN FRANCISCO CHRONICLE

Lecture delivered October 28, 1936

THE POLICY OF THE UNITED STATES IN THE PACIFIC AND THE FAR EAST

AMERICAN RELATIONS in the Pacific and with the Orient, it is trite to point out, represent not one aspect of a unified foreign policy, but one of three seemingly almost unrelated policies. Briefly, these policies have been, toward Europe, nonentanglement; toward Latin America, the Monroe Doctrine; and toward Asia, the Open Door.

Our practice, to be sure, has by no means consistently complied with these simple theories. Toward Europe, for instance, the theory of no entanglements has not prevented the United States from being not merely "entangled," but actually engaged as a belligerent, in the only two general wars which Europe has had since the thirteen colonies became a nation. If we were not involved in the intervening isolated wars, neither were some of the European nations. The United States was not in the Crimean War, but neither was Spain. It had no part in the wars of Prussia against Austria in 1866 or against France in 1871, but neither had Britain. The only wars which did spread over Europe—the Napoleonic wars and the recent World War—also involved this country. Neither of those wars settled the only issue which brought us into them, namely, our particular doctrine of the freedom of the seas, and that issue still remains, to drag us into the next general European war unless we revise beforehand the policy which drew us into both the others. Nonentanglement in Europe has remained a theory which has effectively restrained the United States from coöperating to prevent European wars, but has not kept it out of them when they occurred.

Similarly, in Latin America, the Monroe Doctrine, which was at first merely a warning to the colonizing imperialist nations of Europe that they must not seek again to extend their system to this hemisphere, became in its second period the pretext for a considerable degree of imperialistic intervention by the United States. The Doctrine did not deter us from a war of conquest on Mexico and, later, on the remaining Spanish possessions, nor from establishing for a time what were regarded as unwelcome protectorates, at least in Central America and the Caribbean region. Now, happily, we are reverting to the original Doctrine, but we are making it a joint policy rather than a unilateral declaration. The extension to South America of our theory toward Europe of nonintervention made us, unfortunately, an obstacle on this hemisphere, as we had already been in Europe, to any effective system of collective security even among the American republics.

Ultimately, the Open Door policy, which was in form a mere demand for equal rights of trade, had added to it the political doctrine of the inviolability of the territorial and administrative integrity of China. This led us to literally entangling alliances in Asia, and with European Powers at that. But when the time came to make good in action the engagements of that alliance, we, like our European allies, failed to do so, and reduced it to a paper document of academic protest, at the only time that it was ever challenged by a major Power resolutely bent on violating it.

Thus, while we still cling to the three contrasting theories, the practical result is that our nonentanglement theory has not kept us out of entanglement in Europe and it has kept us from constructive coöperation in Latin America and Asia, where, in theory, it does not apply.

These contrasts between our theories and the inconsistencies of our practice, with respect to the three major regions of the earth, are doubtless familiar. It may not be so generally realized that in the earlier stages of our relations with the Far East we had two policies, one toward China and another toward Japan. In China, on the one hand, we waited for the aggression to be done by the other Powers, notably England, and then took advantage of the most-favored-nation principle to assume for ourselves whatever benefits their aggressions extorted from China. In Japan, on the other hand, we took the aggressive lead and the other Powers came in for our benefits under the same favored-nation rule. It is a coincidence, perhaps, or a paradox, but at any rate an interesting fact, that the aggressions of America on Japan have been treated by Japan as constructive and helpful, but the aggressions in China of other Powers, by which we incidentally benefited, have, by the Chinese, been considered restrictive and they still resent them.

Also, the theoretical basis of our policy toward China has always been trade, though it eventuated in what amounted to political commitments. The purpose of our first aggression in Japan may have been political, but it produced in Japan the most remarkable political, social, and economic transformation that has taken place in any nation in modern times. Our trade relations with Japan are a major factor now, but in the beginning they were quite a minor one.

It is also necessary to recognize that the Spanish and Philippine wars, which made the United States an Asiatic Power, and the World War, which marked the end of one era and the beginning of another for us as for all other nations, of necessity also divided our Asiatic policy into the same distinctly separate periods.

Another curious fact is that the very cause which precipitated our policy of isolation from Europe also opened our markedly different intercourse with the Orient. Before the American Revolution, the American colonists had taken a very active part in British commerce and had built and operated much of the British merchant marine. After the Revolution, the Navigation Act and other embargoes long handicapped us in European and even in Caribbean trade, and drove us to seek other outlets. So our merchant vessels went eastward around the Cape of Good Hope and westward around Cape Horn, into the Pacific which the Spaniards had previously partly explored and mapped and where our whalers had already pioneered the way. Thus we sought in far Cathay what we had lost in Europe and the Caribbean.

Following some earlier voyages from New England ports, the first vessel from New York to Canton, in 1784, also carried the first American representative to China. There were, of course, at that time no official diplomatic relations between proud China and the inferior foreign barbarians, but Major Samuel Shaw, supercargo of that vessel, the *Empress of China,* was elected by Congress, upon the recommendation of Foreign Minister Jay, "Commissioner" at Canton. Thus our semidiplomatic relations in China began even before the Constitution was adopted, under the Articles of Confederation. Shaw was reappointed by President Washington and he and his successors for many years remained our commercial representatives in China. They were all merchants doing business at Canton, and their public functions were incidental.

Previous to the so-called "Opium War" of Great Britain, from 1839 to 1842, all our intercourse in China was purely mercantile. There were no treaties, but China had grudgingly conceded to the British and others certain trading rights in Canton. These persons were required to live on a sand spit in the Pearl River—the island of Shameen where the foreign quarter still is—and to deal exclusively with certain Cantonese Cohongs or merchant guilds. They could have no communication with the government, whose mandarins regarded them and their sordid occupation of trade as beneath contempt, but they might present "petitions" to the hong heads, who transmitted them or not, as they pleased, and if they were transmitted, they were read or not by the officials, as they pleased. It was a free field for whoever could get the best of it, in the bargainings of Chinese trade, and the shrewd Yankees did not come out the worst.

In the light of the demands of modern China to be treated by other nations as an equal, it is significant to recall that until 1860 Europe and the United States were struggling to be recognized by the Chinese on terms even remotely approaching equality. The Chinese, like the ancient Greeks, divided the world into themselves and the barbarians. They conceded to the barbarians only the right of paying tribute to the Emperor, and they required that representatives of the barbarians, whom they termed "tribute bearers," prostrate themselves in "kowtow" on the floor before him, in token of inferiority and submission.

In addition, the earlier representatives of our government were all merchants, seeking trade, and in the China of that time business held so despicable a status and merchants were so inferior a caste, that they were considered to be not worth the notice of cultured government officials.

The breaking down of this barrier of Chinese pride was left mainly to the British. The United States, seeking only trade, was content to gather up the crumbs of privilege which fell from the British table. As early as 1793, Lord McCartney had tried to establish diplomatic relations with the Chinese Court, and by a show of force he managed actually to be received in the presence of the great Manchu Emperor Chien Lung without performing the kowtow, but the negotiations came to nothing. In 1816, Lord Amherst again undertook to open direct negotiations with the Throne, but was not admitted when he refused to perform the kowtow. In 1823, Lord Napier went on a similar errand, but had no success.

Previous to the "Opium War," all business had to be done in Canton. After that war, in 1842, Hongkong was ceded to Britain and four more treaty ports were opened. Commodore Kearny of the American fleet managed to get from the Chinese Commissioner a most-favored-nation agreement under which Americans received the same port privileges. The question of extraterritoriality did not come up until later.

After the British, in 1842, had forced on China a treaty that not only recognized their commercial rights, but also granted the unprecedented privilege of stationing a resident representative at Peking with access to the Throne, Caleb Cushing, the American representative, sought a similar treaty, but the best he could do was to negotiate with the Commissioner of the Emperor, on Portuguese soil at Macao, an agreement granting better trade conditions, similar to those obtained by the British, and also establishing the new principle of extraterritoriality. This principle of extraterritoriality has held ever since, and in recent years has been the cause of much Chinese dissatisfaction. In the beginning it was as much a favor to the Chinese, who did not want to be troubled with the affairs of foreigners, as to the Americans. The American treaty, however, differed from the British treaty in declaring the opium trade illegal and in renouncing all claim of protection to Americans engaged in opium smuggling. This was a virtuous gesture of idealism, but it did not stop the smuggling; the next treaty with China, instead of prohibiting the trade, undertook to limit it.

Thus, before 1850 a beginning had been made by both Europe and the United States in commercial and diplomatic relations with China. For the next decade or more, further progress was checked by the Crimean War in Europe and by the great Taiping Rebellion in China. The chaos in China made the execution of even the rights granted by the earlier treaties practically inoperative, and as soon as Europe was again able to turn its attention to China the European Powers generally were favorable to extorting concessions by force.

America's policy was to coöperate with those Powers in everything except the coercion and then to claim for America whatever the others got by that coercion.

In 1857, under Lord Elgin, another British war in China began. Finally, in 1858, after the bombardment and capture of Canton and the reduction of the Taku forts below Tientsin, Lord Elgin forced the first really modern relations with China. The American representative tried to negotiate at Peking for similar concessions, but was refused audience because of refusal to kowtow. He finally negotiated a treaty with subordinates in another place. In 1860, Lord Elgin, with a larger force, got his final concessions and the United States came aboard under the most-favored-nation clause.

Thus ends, in 1860, the first period of our relations with China. Since then, foreigners have dictated to China, not China to the foreigners.

In the partly parallel story of Japan, it is interesting to note the coincidences of dates between the development of American expansion at home and the beginnings of American expansion still farther westward across the Pacific.

Westward the course of empire still took its way, nor did it stop at our Pacific coast. With our backs toward Europe we could maintain the fiction of isolation across the Atlantic, but with our faces turned westward the pursuit of a similar isolation policy in that direction apparently never occurred to anybody. The only trace of it was directed against any sort of coöperation with European nations whom we found in the Pacific. We had no hesitation in interfering with Asiatic affairs, but there were only a few exceptions to our policy of doing our interfering alone. Some of those instances, however, have been of decisive historical importance.

From the beginning until 1848, American imperialism had taken the form of a vast continental expansion. As an agricultural people which wanted more land, we proceeded to take it. But an industrial and commercial people seeks expansion in markets rather than in territory, and when, at the close of the Mexican War, our great continental domain was completed and consolidated, we were ready to seek an ever larger market expansion—to which, however, Commodore Perry's opening of Japan in 1852–54 was only incidental.

The next coincidental date was 1867, immediately following our Civil War. In that year the United States acquired Alaska, Canada became the second American federal continental commonwealth, and Japan, through the abdication of the Shogun and the restoration of the temporal power of the Emperor, emerged from a medieval feudal state to a modern unified nation.

The next date is 1898, when the United States fought the Spanish War, and through the taking of the Philippines and the annexation of Hawaii became a Pacific Power. This date immediately followed the Sino-Japanese War of 1895, from which Japan first emerged as a World Power; it immediately preceded the letter of John Hay which sought to establish the principle of the Open Door in China in 1899. It preceded, too, the Boxer Rebellion of 1900, which riveted new international shackles on China and ushered in the final decade of the Manchu dynasty, which culminated in its fall in 1911 and the beginning of a new era in China.

The next Japanese war, with Russia in 1904–05, which definitely established Japan as a great World Power, coincided with the dominance in the United States of Theodore Roosevelt, one of the few American statesmen who managed successfully to make America an active participant in world affairs. Some of the aspects of his part in the Treaty of Portsmouth, which ended the Russo-Japanese War, are still in dispute. There may be time to go into that later.

To revert to Japan, it is interesting to conjecture what might have been the consequences on this continent if, during the entire period of American expansion, Japan had not pursued exactly the contrary policy. The voluntary closing of Japan to all foreign intercourse coincided almost exactly with the landing of the Pilgrims at Plymouth and ended just after the completion of our territorial expansion to the Pacific, following the Mexican War. For these more than two centuries, Japan, formerly a maritime and trading nation, had closed all doors to the outside world except the small, closely guarded aperture of a Dutch trading station at Nagasaki. All that time the western half of the United States was open to whoever might choose to take it. That Japan, if open, would have participated in the world-wide mechanical and commercial progress is demonstrated by its achievements as soon as its doors were opened. They had been closed for quite other reasons than any prejudice against this particular aspect of Western life. Japanese colonization of the American West would have been easily within the capacity of the Japan that appeared immediately following its opening, and would have come long before Americans could have competed with, or

Mexicans have resisted, that colonization. But when Japan's opening came, the United States had completed the occupation of its great western domain and had established securely the Pacific Coast as the western frontier of Occidental civilization and of the white man's world. It is easily possible, if not almost probable, that otherwise the western half of the United States would now be Oriental in race and in institutions, and that the eastern half alone would have been an outpost of Europe, which perhaps would never have declared its political independence and certainly would never have attained its present importance.

Japan's recent history has been curiously divided into periods of almost exactly ten years, each of which has also corresponded to an important epoch in American policy. I have already referred to the two wars of 1895 and 1905. Ten years later, in 1915, when the World War was in progress, came the famous Twenty-One Demands on China, which have been the foundation of all subsequent Japanese policy. American diplomacy was in no small degree influential in securing the suspension of the worst of those demands, but the world has had to deal with their recrudescence ever since. Not quite ten years later came the Washington Conference of 1922, which established a whole series of multilateral treaties involving the United States and Europe in the Orient, and only nine years afterward the Manchuran incident of 1931 smashed not only those treaties but also the whole system of collective security in the world and ushered in the present era of fearful, hurried, and costly rearmament and preparations for universal war.

On the opening of Japan in 1854 by Commodore Perry, I must resist the temptation to too much storytelling. One of my treasured possessions is a copy of the first edition of Commodore Perry's report of the expedition, and one of my cherished recollections is that of my long acquaintance with Viscount Shibusawa, the last survivor in Japan of those who actually saw the "black ships" arrive and took active part in the events of the time. I have heard him describe the scene and also recount how the high character and fine personality of Townsend Harris, the first American consul, converted him from a militant antiforeign agitator to a lifelong friend of the United States. To have seen as much history in Europe as Shibusawa lived through in Japan, one would have to be five hundred years old. With these relations on both sides, I feel almost like a second-hand personal observer of this historic event.

Suffice it to say that, by a mixture of diplomacy and show of force, Perry did open the long-closed door of Japan and secured the right of asylum for shipwrecked American sailors. The commercial concessions of this first treaty were negligible, but four years later a treaty between Townsend Harris and the Shogun Iyesada opened real opportunities for trade and residence.

A decade of transition followed, at the end of which the Shogunate and feudalism disappeared, the temporal power of the Emperor was restored, under the young Meiji Emperor Mutsuhito, and modern Japan began. It was not until 1889, however, that the liberal Constitution was granted, and not until 1894, the year of the Sino-Japanese War, that full reciprocal equality of rights between Japan and foreign Powers was attained.

From that time on, the relations of the United States with China and Japan were more intimately interrelated. After the Sino-Japanese War, ostensibly fought to protect the "independence" of Korea, European Powers interfered to deprive Japan of the fruits of victory, and then straightway proceeded to do in China, without even the title of conquest, what they had prevented Japan from doing after a successful war. They waited until America's back was turned, in the Spanish War, to begin the dividing up of China into "spheres of influence," contrary to our traditional principle of equal commercial rights, which John Hay was soon to make historic under the name of the "Open Door." But the United States emerged from the war with Spain as also an Asiatic Power, and very much interested.

The famous Open Door note of September, 1899, was both more and less than it seemed. It was good American politics to pretend that it was the act of America alone, but it seems certain that the initiative was at least shared by Lord Charles Beresford. Hay would have been glad to make it a definite alliance between Great Britain, the United States, and Japan to safeguard the integrity of China. He had the scholar's contempt for the demagogues of politics, and, as he said on a related matter a little later, "that we should be compelled to refuse the assistance of the greatest power in the world, in carrying out our own policy, because all Irishmen are Democrats and some Germans are fools—is enough to drive a man mad."

So the note was issued by the United States alone, and all the Powers were shamed into replies which Hay chose to construe as acceptances, though he knew that the "reservations" attached to some of them made them fall far short of "acceptances."

Almost immediately thereafter there followed the Boxer Rebellion and the siege of the legations in Peking, and the United States made one of its rare exceptions to the rule of pretending never to take joint action with anybody. Our troops took part with those of Japan, Russia, Great Britain, and France in the relief of Peking and we joined in the negotiations for the protocol of the following year. Secretary Hay defined the attitude of the United States on the Chinese question in language which has become historic, and which was embodied, with only slight change, in the later nine-power treaty of 1922: "The policy of the government of the United States is to seek a solution which may bring about permanent safety and peace to China, preserve Chinese territorial and administrative entity, protect all rights guaranteed to friendly powers by treaty and international law, and safeguard for the world the principle of equal and impartial trade with all parts of the Chinese Empire."

Thus we became committed in principle to a policy toward China which was political as well as commercial. But no one knew better than John Hay that if the time ever came when the only way to maintain the political part of this commitment was to fight for it, we would not do so.

The very next year after the Boxer protocol, which we used our influence to make as mild as possible, Russia set the example of treaty violation which has marked the relations of the Powers to China ever since. It retained in Manchuria the troops it had agreed to withdraw, and thus menaced both China and Japan. This led to the Anglo-Japanese Alliance, which lasted for the next twenty years, until it was ended at the Washington Conference. Its first effect was to release Japan from the fear of intervention by other Powers if it used force on Russia, which it proceeded to do in the war of 1904–05.

This war again brought the United States into active participation in the affairs of the Far East. The peace negotiations were initiated ostensibly by President Theodore Roosevelt, but actually at the wish of Japan, and the Treaty of Portsmouth, which ended the war, was negotiated and signed in this country with Roosevelt as its godfather.

Roosevelt's actual part in the negotiations, as well as in the concurrent troubles of Europe, in which he himself thought that he had prevented a world war, has been a subject of so much dispute that I will not take your time to go into it. One recent aspect of it, however, I will mention, partly on account of a minor personal incident which, because it has been nowhere written, ought perhaps to be put on record.

In 1932, the secret memoirs of Viscount Kaneko were published, in which the statement was made that, during the negotiations for the Portsmouth treaty of 1905, President Roosevelt had advocated a "Japanese Monroe Doctrine" and had promised that, if Japan would proclaim such a doctrine, he would support it, in or out of office. The intent of the publication of this statement in Japan was to attribute to

Roosevelt support of what Japan now calls the Asiatic Monroe Doctrine. Actually, no doubt, the statement was the exact reverse of that. Japan was supposedly protecting the independence of Korea and of Manchuria and the integrity of China, as we were protecting the independence of Latin American states, and as John Hay would have been glad to join with Japan and England in doing in Asia. The existing Japanese Asiatic Monroe Doctrine, on the contrary, proclaims the right of Japan to destroy all these independences. The fact that Roosevelt in fact never carried out his reported promise to support the doctrine across the Pacific indicates, if anything, that he was soon disillusioned with respect to its real intent.

I knew both Theodore Roosevelt and Kaneko, but I will relate only an amusing incident which illustrates nothing more than Kaneko's continued pride in his association with Roosevelt.

I was in Tokyo at the time of the great chaos of the earthquake of 1923, and, with characteristic Japanese imperturbability, Viscount Shibusawa insisted on giving me a formal luncheon in what was left of the Bankers' Club, to which he invited such of the elite of Japan as his messengers could find in the confusion. Kaneko did not come, and sent excuses which were obvious subterfuges. I found out afterward that the real reason was that he had lost all his clothes in the fire except the old kimono in which he escaped, and he would not appear at the Bankers' Club in that. When I called on him afterward, at his son-in-law's house, and found him still garbed in the same kimono, he told me how he had lost everything in his house except the portraits of the Emperor and of Theodore Roosevelt, which he had risked his life and sacrificed his clothes and furniture to save. Such things can happen, in Japan.

Skipping intermediate matters, which would be included in a complete history, we now come to the Washington Conference of 1922, which ended the Anglo-Japanese Alliance, established a tentative naval limitation, and made an enlarged Hay doctrine toward China a matter of formal multilateral treaty and official international law. This, too, was one of the rare but important occasions when we took joint instead of separate action in the Orient.

The Great War and the Treaty of Versailles had intervened; the Twenty-One Demands had been served on China and partly withdrawn, but those affecting Manchuria were aggressively maintained; the Anglo-Japanese Alliance was threatening trouble between Britain and the Dominions; China and Japan had both been disappointed in the provisions of the treaty; the United States had been in controversy with Japan over the Japanese mandated islands (concernng whose earlier history I could tell some stories which I think have never been written), and the whole world was engaged in a frantic naval race. The United States had refused to ratify the treaty of Versailles and had negotiated a separate treaty on the characteristic Senate attitude of claiming all rights and recognizing no duties under it, and had refused to join the League. But here was this multitude of matters which had to be settled somehow, and in which we were directly concerned, but which we would not settle through the League because it was contaminated with the "Europe" in which we still imagined we had had no part, even though the last of our soldiers were not yet back from the great war there in which we had participated. So there was nothing for us to do but to hold an international conference of our own on these matters, which, because it was held on American soil, we could imagine was a purely American affair. In some respects, that part of the American mind which is represented by the Senatorial isolationists is almost as naïve as the China of Chien Lung.

The story of the conference is too recent to need detailed recounting, and the part concerning naval limitation does not directly concern us here, except in respect to the controversy over the 5–5–3 ratio with Japan, and the reasons, both ways, for that ratio.

As the outcome of the conference, China got back Shantung, not by conference action but by a separate external agreement between the Chinese and the Japanese delegates; the Anglo-Japanese Alliance was ended, and new four-power and nine-power agreements substituted; the capital ships of the navies were limited to a number which was intended, in the Pacific, to make a direct naval war between Japan and the United States across the Pacific physically impossible; the various minor disputes were adjusted; all parties agreed not to fortify their island possessions in the West Pacific, and, most important of all, the nine-power treaty was signed, in which the Powers pledged themselves: (1) to respect the sovereignty, the independence, and the territorial and administrative integrity of China; (2) to provide the fullest and most unembarrassed opportunity to China to develop and maintain for itself an effective and stable government; (3) to use their influence for the purpose of effectually establishing and maintaining the principle of equal opportunity for the commerce and industry of all nations throughout the territory of China; and (4) to refrain from taking advantage of conditions in China in order to seek special rights or privileges which would abridge the rights of subjects or citizens of friendly States, and from countenancing action inimical to the security of such States.

To this was afterward added the Kellogg Pact, applicable to the Far East as well as elsewhere, in which the nations renounced war as an instrument of national policy and agreed to seek the settlement of all disputes, without exception, by pacific means only.

These nine-power engagements, in which Japan joined, to respect the integrity of China, were the political consideration for which Britain and the United States consented to a naval limitation which left them powerless to protect that integrity.

If these engagements had been kept, the problem of peace in the Far East would have been solved and the machinery of peace in Europe would today be intact.

It was the breaking of these engagements, in Manchuria, in 1931, which made inoperative, and perhaps has destroyed, the system of collective security throughout the world, and which brought on the present era of frantic preparation for expected universal war.

On this, too, I must resist the temptation to storytelling.

For I happened to be on the spot and saw it happen; I was in Mukden dealing openly with the Japanese military authorities and secretly with the Chinese, and slipping information over the diplomatic wires to our government and through other channels to the League; I was, soon afterward, in Shanghai and Nanking, in direct contact with the Chinese government and in daily touch, by means of the Chinese government radio, with the Secretariat of the League; later I had surprisingly frank talks with the Japanese Foreign Office in Tokyo, and after my return I had frequent and close contacts with the State Department and the White House on the American part of the subsequent negotiations. One who has been so close as that to all parts of an epochal historic event is simply overwhelmed with the abundance of his material, and the only way not to say too much, at this hour of the night, is to say nothing.

You all know the collapse that followed: how the League, with the United States participating and often leading, always *said* the right thing just too late, and refrained from *doing* anything; how the verdict of the League, with its acceptance of the Stimson nonrecognition doctrine, has isolated Japan ever since; how Japan walked out of the League and was later followed by Germany when it, too, wished to violate treaties; how Italy was emboldened to the same course and thereby precipitated the present impotence, panic, and chaos of Europe; how Japan has gone steadily and ruthlessly ahead, in the conquest and virtual annexation of Manchuria and the gradual penetration and domination of China, and how this has eventuated in new alliances and counteralliances, which guarantee that any serious disturbance in either Europe or Asia will at once involve the other continent and make difficult the nonparticipation of America; and how, from this beginning, the sanctity of treaties, the honor of the pledged word, and all good will and good faith have gone out of the relations of nations.

All this from an incident in Mukden, on September 18, 1931, so small that I have never seen a printed account of it in any book or newspaper which described how small it really was!

That, too, is now behind us. The conquest of Manchuria, like that of Ethiopia, is a *fait accompli*. The world is now challenged by the three "have not" powers, Germany, Italy, and Japan, all overpopulated and lacking colonies to provide them in peace the expansion they think they need, or to accept the certainty that they will seek to take it by war. And America, with all its new mania for isolation, is challenged either to face that challenge and participate in the joint efforts for its solution, or else to surrender all its traditional policy of the Open Door and the integrity of China, and all its naval policy of the freedom of the seas.

We cannot escape that challenge by closing our eyes and ears to it and wishing it did not exist. Neither can we meet it by waiting until the explosion actually bursts on us. To discuss this question more fully would be to pass from history to politics. I can therefore do no more than remind you that we are still in the midst of the problems the antecedents and background of which I have all too superficially sketched; and that the possible consequences of our doing no better in the immediate future than we have done in the recent past may be great enough to stagger the imagination, as we contemplate them now, and perhaps to shake the world, if and when they happen.

THE TWO ROADS: ISOLATION OR COLLECTIVE SECURITY

FRANK M. RUSSELL
PROFESSOR OF POLITICAL SCIENCE
IN THE UNIVERSITY OF CALIFORNIA

Lecture delivered November 4, 1936

THE TWO ROADS: ISOLATION OR COLLECTIVE SECURITY

IN THE DISCUSSION of this controversial question I am happy, at the point of departure, at any rate, to take a position that is not likely to be assailed from any quarter. The two great objectives of American foreign policy which most truly reflect the aspirations of the people of the United States are peace and security. This has never been truer than at present. The neutrality legislation enacted within the last year (1935) in response to a strong popular demand that measures should be taken calculated to keep the United States out of war, eloquently testifies to the present temper of the people. Certain foreign dictators, intoxicated with a brief moment of power, may strut belligerently across the world stage and declaim loudly upon the "absurdity of permanent peace" and the ennobling and purifying effects of war, but they arouse nothing but disapproval and distrust in a country whose habits and traditions predispose it to prefer votes to violence in the adjustment of conflicting claims and the determination of public policies. It must not be forgotten that the most vigorous and sustained peace movement in the world developed in this country in the hundred years before the outbreak of the World War, and that the United States was in the vanguard of those nations which promoted the employment of arbitration for the settlement of international disputes and looked forward eventually to the establishment of a permanent international court of justice.

We are modest enough, I hope, to admit that this preference

for pacific settlement as well as our relatively infrequent participation in war, were not due to any inherent ethical superiority of the American people—for we are, after all, for the most part the descendants of transplanted Europeans. Rather is it to be attributed to that "detached and distant situation" of which Washingon spoke, to the absence of powerful and ambitious neighbors, to a vast and well-endowed domain capable of absorbing our energies in the pursuits of peace, and finally to wise political leadership. It is also to be noted that we have never been a peace-at-any-price nation, nor have we fought merely for the defense of our country against attack. Three of our four wars since Independence have been fought on foreign soil. We have always been a spirited people and, to others on occasion, we have seemed arrogant and aggressive as well. Perhaps our sporadic militancy may be mainly attributed to the bumptious and venturesome spirit of youth, for "America's youth," as has been remarked, "is one of her oldest and most hallowed traditions." Be that as it may, meekness has not been one of our outstanding characteristics, and idealism has not always won the day against materialism in our relations with the outside world. These facts must be given their due weight in any discussion of the recently much debated question, "Can the United States stay out of war?"

Isolation and self-containment as a fundamental state policy is not an indigenous American idea conceived by George Washington and rediscovered for the American people by Senator Borah. It was attempted as a deliberate and more or less reasoned policy more than two thousand years ago in

Greece. Ancient Sparta, physically isolated from other states to an unusual degree, followed for a time a policy of abstention from peaceful intercourse with these states, while at the same time preparing for war against them. In the pursuit of this policy commercial intercourse with citizens of other communities was forbidden, foreigners were expelled, and Spartans were not allowed to travel abroad. In the realm of Western philosophic thought Plato was perhaps the first thoroughgoing isolationist. The ideal state, according to the conception he gives us in the *Laws,* was one so situated that it would be tempted to engage in as little intercourse with other states as possible. It should not be on the seacoast, for it would then have an urge to develop trade and commerce, and its citizens would consequently acquire luxurious and depraved tastes and a greed for wealth. As far as possible it should be self-contained and economically independent of other states. It would thus be in a position to perfect its own institutions and provide its citizens with the ideal conditions for living the good life undistracted by wars and disturbances from the outside, and uncontaminated by the lust for wealth and power. This ideal of political and economic self-sufficiency was not exclusively a Platonian conception. It was basic in the Greek philosophy of the State. But the centrifugal forces of life were against it and, in any event, the small city-state was not capable of affording security from without in an age which accepted

> The well-tried simple plan
> That they should take who have the power
> And they should keep who can.

The ideal, however, has been revived from time to time. Johann Fichte, the German philosopher, writing toward the end of the eighteenth century, advocated *The Closed Commercial State,* which should shut its frontiers to foreign trade and seek to realize economic self-sufficiency. This would enable it to avoid wars and develop a completely distinctive national life. But Fichte was not a king, he was only a philosopher, and no such state emerged. Could it have been realized in any event? Probably not. At any rate, the century immediately following his ambitious proposal saw an unprecedented development of international trade, and national states were swept in the direction opposite to that of self-containment.

In recent years, however, the national policies of states throughout the world have reflected a disposition to seek economic self-sufficiency, if not political isolation, for reasons pointed out in one of the earlier lectures in the present volume. One need not labor the argument that, as far as most states are concerned, the ideal of autarchy, never attained by any important state of the past, cannot be even approximately realized in the economically interdependent world of today. There are those, however, who contend that the United States, because of its geographical position, the extent of its territory, the abundance of its resources, and the ingenuity of its people, is in a position to succeed with the experiment. Moreover, it is argued, this is the only road to the security which we seek and to the peace to which we aspire. It is likewise, so we are told, the only road to internal stability and an assured and abiding prosperity. Foreign markets are uncertain markets, foreign investments insecure investments, and foreign products are neither necessary nor desirable if domestic products can be substituted. Moreover, it is asserted that international trade, involving a struggle for markets, does not make for peace; it is one of the basic causes of international friction and war. We do not understand the world beyond our own borders, and we cannot control it. But we can establish controls within our own frontiers; we can, if we choose, insulate ourselves from the disturbing effects of fluctuating foreign currencies and the devastating consequences of foreign wars by staying at home and "cultivating our own garden." Have our cotton growers in the past depended upon foreign markets for the absorption of more than 50 per cent of the amount that they produce? The answer is, restrict the acreage for the growing of cotton to an amount necessary to satisfy domestic needs. Have we exported 40 per cent of our tobacco, 20 per cent of our wheat, and 40 per cent of our machinery? Very well. Reduce acreages and output, and turn our economic energies in other directions. Let us utilize the depression, which has already caused the loss of much of this as well as much of the rest of our foreign trade, to plan a national economy which will give us a balanced economic national life, and afford the maximum of independence of the rest of the world. On the political side, those taking this position would warn us to abstain in the future from such acts of knight errantry as took us into the war to "make the world safe for democracy." And, according to some, but not to all, who advocate this policy, we should likewise liquidate our overseas colonial responsibilities, abandon the defense of

American commercial and financial interests abroad, including the policy of the Open Door, and thereby be in a position to reduce our armed establishment to a point sufficient only to protect our continental territory and uphold the Monroe Doctrine.

This is the road of isolation and self-containment. Shall we set out upon it? Apparently it leads to those things demanded, on the one hand, by American materialism, and, on the other, by American idealism. If we restrict our imports to products not capable of being grown or manufactured in this country, as is contemplated, our producers for the home market will be freed from foreign competition and will therefore be in a better position to command higher prices. If the consumer has to pay more for these products, higher wage scales, it is asserted, will put him in a position to do so without hardship. A thoroughgoing isolationist policy is, likewise, calculated to make a strong appeal to American pacifism and idealism. The American people entered the World War because great numbers of them had come to believe that the cause of democracy and freedom was at stake, and that the menace of autocracy must be removed. Pacifists and liberals for the most part gave their support, hoping that it was a "war to end war," and that an organization of the world for peace would be realized at its conclusion. Those generous hopes were disappointed. Vindictiveness and greed permeated the settlement, obscuring or vitiating even those parts that were good. Disillusioned and chagrined, many American liberals, as well as other groups in the country, returned a blanket indictment of Versailles and all its works, rejecting the good along with the bad. Like the philosopher, Candide, who in his travels had found the world unwilling to listen to reason, but cruel and stupid and irrational, many Americans decided it was best to return to the cultivation of our own garden. Actually, however, the withdrawal was only partial. We did not join the League or accept membership in the World Court, but we did push American trade and investments in all parts of the world, and we even entered into political arrangements with other Powers for the protection of our interests and the advancement of our policies in the Pacific and the Far East. But with the setting in of the Great Depression, which we likewise attributed, by oversimplification, to the War, the Peace, and the unwise postwar policies of others, many were ready for a more complete withdrawal from the world and for an experiment with the policy of self-containment. American liberalism, thwarted in its attempt to spread enlightenment abroad, can, at any rate, it was said, make its ideals come true within the more limited area under our own control. By cultivating our own garden we can, according to this view, not only assure American security and increase American well-being, but we can also build a model commonwealth which may set a standard for the rest of the world.

This attractive picture of domestic contentment, painted by the "Why quit our own?" philosophers of the *Saturday Evening Post,* and disseminated by the Chemical Foundation, needs further examination. Does it mean that we are deliberately to plan to eliminate as far as possible our foreign trade? If so, it runs counter to the historic American trade policy going back to the days of George Washington. The Fathers never advised, and their descendants never followed, a policy of commercial isolation. Quite to the contrary, they encouraged foreign commerce, and even deliberately utilized the occasion of European wars to extend that commerce. Whatever the wisdom of that policy, it has been followed for nearly a century and a half; great sections and producing interests have become dependent upon it, and those who would attempt to snuff it out by legislation must undertake to change our traditions, habits, tastes, and the character of our wants, and lay violent hands on the entire national economy. Even as they write, these advocates of political and economic isolation cannot but see that the current is running the other way. Although our combined exports and imports dropped from $9,640,000,000 in 1929 to $2,935,000,000 in 1932, they had already risen to a value of more than $4,280,000,000 in 1935 in spite of restrictive trade policies throughout the world. If this trend is to be halted and a policy of self-containment followed on the assumption that a developing foreign trade will jeopardize our national security, we must be prepared to pay the price. If foreign markets for our cotton, wheat, tobacco, machinery, and many other commodities are cut off, not only these but other industries whose prosperity is dependent upon them will be dislocated, many investors will suffer, and the unemployment problem will be greatly aggravated for an indeterminate period. Assuming that an adjustment is finally made by the artificial diversion of this economic energy into less productive channels,—and this would apparently be necessary,—we should probably have to be content with a lower

standard of living than we have previously enjoyed. Moreover, if such an experiment is attempted, producers and
manufacturers and traders of the country must be prepared
to accept a degree of governmental regimentation and control far greater than they are likely to tolerate unless one
greatly mistakes the temper of the American businessman.
In respect to imports, it is well known that, although the
United States is relatively well endowed with minerals and
raw materials, it lacks altogether or produces in insufficient
quantities a number of commodities now imported which
are essential to our automobile and other industries. Even
if substitutes were found for some of these, it is a question
whether they would not be more costly and less satisfactory.
We may, of course, give up the luxurious habit of riding in
automobiles and let grass grow in the streets of Detroit, but
we are as little likely to do so as we are to give up drinking
tea and coffee, or eating chocolate candy. Nor is it likely
that we are ready to weaken the national defense by giving
up the importation of the twenty-six "strategic products"
listed by the War Department as produced outside the United
States yet indispensable in time of war. Of course a policy of
political isolation and economic self-containment is supposed
to supply the recipe for keeping us out of war. But not only
can there be no guaranty of this; there is reason even to believe
that it would have the opposite effect. Any attempt by the
United States to follow such a policy would give a further
impetus to other states already suffering from policies of economic nationalism to struggle desperately to make themselves economically independent of the outside world. Yet

such a world following the ideal of self-containment inevitably means a world of authoritarian states in which a struggle for dwindling markets, colonies, and essential raw materials will take place, and war between the "haves" and the "have nots" will be assured. Under these conditions no amount of money spent on military defense would guarantee this or any other country against war. What the world needs, if peace is desired, and I think the instincts of plain people everywhere predispose them toward peace, is the leveling, not the further erection of Chinese walls, and the adoption of policies looking toward the maximum circulation of goods rather than measures calculated to build up a series of militant closed states. This is not to say that a world utopia of peace and plenty is to be expected simply by a return to Adam Smith and the classical theories of *laissez faire* in which unplanned and uncontrolled trade, based solely on the enlightened self-interest of individuals, was regarded as the panacea for all the world's economic and political ills. Those theories were based on the assumption of the free competition of individual entrepreneurs extended into the international sphere. Today we live in an era of trusts, combinations, and cartels, many of them not stopping at national frontiers, but extending their control and operations far beyond. Prices tend to be fixed in the light of what the traffic will bear rather than by the higgling of the market. Those doing business across frontiers may be national in their make-up or international in their organization and direction, but perhaps the general tendency is for them to be organized as national producing and trading units, with a national outlook. Under these circumstances both national and international planning in the field of production and trade are indicated for the future. But to be salutary it must point in the direction of the greatest utilization of the world's resources for the good of the peoples, and the consequent development of international trade rather than the cornering of natural resources and the restriction of that trade for the exclusive benefit of nationalist or imperialist systems.

Let us now turn to the question of peace and security in relation to political policy. The first departure from our tradition of political aloofness—I do not say isolation—was not made, as is commonly supposed, at the time of the World War. It occurred in the presidency of Theodore Roosevelt. Not only did he play the rôle of influential mediator and thus affect the terms of settlement of the Russo-Japanese War, but he also acted in other matters concerned with the political, colonial, and commercial rivalries of the Powers in all parts of the world. Unable on account of constitutional limitations, and the traditional policy of the country, to contract alliances in the carrying out of his policies as he would have liked, he nevertheless "took sides" whenever, in his judgment, a question of "righteousness" was involved. In the Far East, acting through his representative, William Howard Taft, he put his seal of approval upon Japan's control of Korea, and received in return an assurance that Japan preferred to have the United States remain in the Philippine Islands. When war in Europe seemed imminent in 1905 over the status of Morocco, Roosevelt was convinced that righteousness was on the side of France and the Entente Powers. He therefore threw his

weight against Germany and Austria, and delivered an ultimatum to the Kaiser which compelled Germany to acquiesce
in a settlement favorable to France. Ostensibly the United
States entered the Morocco Conference because we were a
signatory of the Treaty of Madrid which provided for the
Open Door; actually President Roosevelt was chiefly, if not
exclusively, motivated by a desire to maintain the existing
balance of power as a means of preserving the peace of the
world. His action may have postponed, it did not avert, the
World War. One cannot but feel that, in any event, en-
shrouded in secrecy as it was, and partaking of the nature of
old-style European ultimatum diplomacy as it did, this action
was dangerous and ill advised. It was, however, consistent
with the "Big Stick" philosophy of Roosevelt, and perhaps
to some extent the President's known activity in foreign affairs reflected the attitude of a newly arrived "Great Power"
concerned to make its influence felt in the councils of the
world.

The second conspicuous departure from American aloofness was marked by our entry into the World War. This time,
not only the President but also Congress and the people in
general were convinced that a larger ethical issue, as well as
the question of our own rights as a neutral, was at stake. That
issue was the right of free peoples everywhere to live their
lives secure from the spiritual oppression and moral degrada-
tion of despotism, and relieved of the specter of war, the
natural child of despotism. "The world must be made safe
for democracy." If the peace that was made at the conclusion
of the war did not reflect that generous ideal except in part,

it was not that the ideal itself was unworthy—the fault lay with those who lacked the necessary courage, unselfishness, and imagination to put it ahead of all other national objectives. The judgment, of course, that has been rendered upon the work that they did has been too harsh and sweeping. They and their successors in the postwar years have worked in a confused and distracted atmosphere of hatred and fear. The war had "broken the rhythm of life," not only in the sense that it had dislocated industry, trade, and finance, but also in its wholesale destruction of spiritual values that had, after all, served as an anchor in the era that had closed. At a time when there has been an unprecedented need for clear thought and constructive endeavor, the people of all nations have suffered more or less from a corroding cynicism and a sense of the futility of all attempts to ameliorate the unhappy lot of mankind as a whole.

The views of those who favor a policy of thoroughgoing isolation for the United States, and likewise of those who admit the necessity of some international coöperation but feel that, as far as we are concerned, it should be confined to nonpolitical affairs, have been bred in this atmosphere and nurtured on certain assumptions the complete validity of which should not be accepted without examination. Within recent years the notion has been widely popularized, for example, that modern wars arise simply out of material selfishness, and that the next war will come as a result of the inflexibility of the "haves" in denying a proper place in the economic sun to the "have nots." For the populations of the "have nots," it is said, have no choice but to look to the efficiency of autocratic government, arm themselves, and be in a position to wrest by force from the wealthy nations the lands and resources they need in order to live. As a matter of fact, the clamor for colonies by the autocratic governments of these "hungry" countries seems to be motivated chiefly by considerations of pride, power, and prestige rather than of economic necessity. Even while they point to their surplus population and their need accordingly for more standing room, they are bending every effort to increase the birth rate and thus to aggravate the population problem. All informed persons know quite well that the colonial acquisitions of the nineteenth century were of no value whatsoever as outlets for the surplus population of the possessing countries. Likewise, their trade with these colonies was insignificant, and when the costs of administration and defense are considered, as well as the rivalries that their possession engendered, the colonies can indeed be said to have been economic and political liabilities rather than assets, if the interest of the people as a whole is taken as the criterion. Since the World War, and particularly since the depression, most raw materials have been available at low prices to noncolonial as well as colonial states. To the degree that countries poor in raw materials have found difficulty in acquiring them in the open market, the fault is to be charged mainly to unwise trade and financial policies which have made it difficult for these countries to secure foreign currency wherewith to pay for their purchases abroad. Once more the remedy seems to lie chiefly in opening rather than in closing trade doors, and in agreements looking toward the stabilization of international exchange. These in turn demand a recognition on the part of governments that human welfare is more to be desired than power and prestige. Certain European states have attained this perspective. The Scandinavian countries, for example, though not well endowed with natural resources, have weathered the depression in good shape and have maintained a high standard of living for their peoples. Apparently they have felt no necessity to build up their armaments, contract alliances, and strive for "a place in the sun." They have, on the contrary, given loyal support to the League of Nations and to all intelligent effort to bring order and security in the world and thus promote the general welfare of peoples.

The assumption that all wars can be explained in terms of economic motives is widely held, and has been implicit in much of the discussion of the neutrality bills of the last session of Congress. The Senatorial investigation of the armaments traffic and its inquiry into the situation of the United States as a neutral during the World War resulted in amassing evidence which many people regard as conclusively showing that the house of Morgan, and the armament and other business interests, forced us into war. It is natural for human beings to leap at simple explanations of complex phenomena. It is common for them to seek a scapegoat upon which to heap the blame for their misfortunes. What *were* the reasons for our entry into the World War? In seeking the answer the safest course would seem to be to ascertain the opinions of competent American historians who have carefully and painstakingly investigated this period of our history in an objective manner. These historians do not agree with the economic determinists. The situation, as Professor Seymour, for example, describes it in his volumes on *American Neutrality* and *American Diplomacy during the World War*, seems to show conclusively that the bankers and munitions interests did not play nearly so prominent a part in taking us into the war as is popularly supposed. From the first the country as a whole, excepting sections in which there were large numbers of Germans, tended to be pro-Ally in sentiment, although not in favor of our entrance into the war. In the course of time, owing to a variety of influences, including, if you like, the activities of economic interests in the background, as well as the resumption of German submarine warfare, which shocked the American people and helped to confirm the growing opinion that Germany was willing to go to any lengths to win, the temper of the country became ready for war. Pride, resentment, and, on the part of President Wilson, certainly, a growing sense of moral obligation to ourselves and the world—all these must be taken into account in order to explain our entrance into the war. And one must not lose sight of them when attempting to appraise the value of our recent neutrality legislation as a means of keeping us out of war. Will the prohibition of the exports of arms and other war materials to belligerents be sufficient? Can our peace be secured by "taking the profits out of war?" It is very doubtful. If economic interests are as powerful and controlling as the economic determinists assume, it is quite unlikely that sufficiently drastic legislation could be passed in the first place, and if it could be passed it is highly doubtful whether it could be enforced, especially in view of the fact that it would work a hardship on the community as a whole as well as upon the special interests directly affected. On the other hand, if the lure of the money bags is not the whole story; if men in the mass are powerfully moved by prejudices, sentiments, ideals, in addition to and often divorced from economic considerations, then a policy based solely on the assumption that economic motives are decisive is dangerously insufficient, and cannot be depended upon to keep us out of a general conflict. Nor, in all probability, can any other negative policy which begins to operate only after the event—after war has broken out—guarantee us peace and security.

There is much to be said, therefore, in behalf of a policy designed to aid in preventing war from breaking out in the first place. This is generally admitted except by those who regard wars as "acts of God," or natural phenomena like earthquakes, and therefore beyond the control of man. But American policy since the World War, as well as before, has presumably been based on the conviction that war is manmade and can be eliminated as a method of social adjustment whenever man is determined to do so. The contribution of the United States toward this end since the World War has taken the direction of promoting collective disarmament and working for the "outlawry of war." It has also sought on occasion to use its moral influence on behalf of pacific settlement. The approach to world peace by the road of disarmament is founded on the belief that, on the one hand, so long as the Powers maintain large armed establishments capable of carrying on aggression against one another, so long will mutual fear and distrust poison the atmosphere of international relations and make peace impossible. If, on the other hand, nations will agree to reduce their armaments to a point at which they cannot be used for aggressive purposes, but will be sufficient to protect national frontiers, an atmosphere of confidence, in which peace can flourish, will be created. The Washington Arms Conference of 1921–22, called on the initiative of the United States, worked out a limitation of naval armaments on this theory. The United States also participated in the World Conference on Disarmament called by the League of Nations in 1932, and our delegates worked for a general reduction of armaments based on the same principle. Since the adoption in 1928 of the Kellogg Pact for the Renunciation of War, American foreign policy in general has been based upon this multilateral treaty which has been regarded as a substitute for the League of Nations. Its ultimate origin and inspiration may be traced to the American movement for the outlawry of war which gained headway in the United States after the decision not to enter the League of Nations. As originally conceived, the civilized nations of the world were to be invited to an international conference for the purpose of drawing up a code of international law which would make war a "public crime," and provide for the settlement of all "purely international disputes" by an international court. Thus war would be cut out of the tissue of civilization by a single major legal operation. This legalitarian conception had no prospect of acceptance, of course, by this or any other government, but the Kellogg Pact, which pledges the individual signatories to renounce war as an instrument of national policy, was regarded by the outlawrists as a partial victory, for the signatories of the Pact agreed in effect to abstain henceforth from the use of war except in a clear case of self-defense.

Now what may be said concerning the efficacy of these policies as applied specifically to the prevention of war? Frankly, one cannot see that they have had any appreciable effect. The efforts to secure a reduction of the weapons of war and of fighting forces has failed, and bigger and better armaments are now the order of the day, the United States being up among the leaders as far as expenditures are concerned. And as for the Kellogg Pact, the signatories bent on aggressive war as an instrument of national policy have paid not the slightest attention to the treaty. These are the facts. What is the explanation? With respect to national armaments, it is perhaps not to be expected that progress will be made toward their abandonment, at any rate as far as the Great Powers are concerned, until it is realized that a satisfactory substitute must be found to accomplish the purposes for which they are designed. What are these purposes? Primarily, armaments are for the defense of national territories and possessions. How much armament will be needed for this purpose by any particular state? Do you ask the state itself? You will get one answer. Do you ask its neighbors? You will get another. Whichever state we may be considering is certain to feel that its safety absolutely requires more armament than the others will admit is necessary. A common yardstick cannot be found for measuring competitive armaments in relation to one another. What armament is necessary for a nation, therefore, becomes a subjective matter which each nation feels it must decide for itself. This is all the more certain to be the case when we consider that armament is also still looked upon by the Great Powers as the most important weapon in the arsenal of diplomacy. The success of a nation's diplomacy is regarded as depending in the last analysis upon the size of its military establishment. Thus armament is not only for defense; it is for the protection of national interests, the promotion of national policies, and the maintenance of national prestige. The conclusion to which one is forced, therefore, is this: as long as nations feel that they must rely upon themselves alone for the defense of their territories, and for the safeguarding of their interests they are not likely to give up the means for doing so. But the Kellogg Pact was confidently expected by many Americans to pave the way for the reduction of armaments to a defensive basis because war was no longer to be used as an instrument of national policy, and therefore armaments large enough to enable nations to employ war for that purpose had no longer any moral justification. The fundamental weakness of the Kellogg Pact, however, lies in the fact that each nation is allowed to interpret the treaty for itself and determine its own obligations under it without fear of any consequences even for a clear violation. For isolation sentiment in the United States was sufficiently strong at the time it was negotiated to prevent the adoption of any means of impartial interpretation or any machinery of enforcement. Desiring peace, but not wanting to involve ourselves in any collective effort to uphold it, we hoped that we might rely for the observance of the Pact upon the good faith of the signatories, and the restraining influence of public opinion. Time has shown that we can count on neither.

Let us now turn to a consideration of certain fundamentals. Ultimately—and I think there will be no disagreement here—the peace and security of nations, the United States included, must depend upon the development and universal acceptance of a system of international law which will be a true expression of the common will for justice in international affairs. Within free states the peace and security of the citizen is guaranteed in precisely this way, the citizen normally looking to the community for the protection of his life and property, and to established legal processes for the settlement of his disputes and the vindication of his rights. The system of liberty under law is not perfect—no legal or political system ever will be; but we all recognize that in democratic states it affords a degree of freedom and security attainable in no other way, and it is difficult to see how nations can hope to find any other road to the peace and security which most of them desire. The real issue today which nations must face is, in the final analysis, the issue of democracy and law versus despotism and violence. Let me explain just what I mean and the bearing it has on the entire thesis that I am supporting.

Democracy may mean many different things, but above all else it signifies a way of life. It recognizes the worth and dignity of human beings as such and the sanctity of human life; it emphasizes the similarities that bind men together rather than the differences that separate them. Ideally, it does not draw invidious distinctions between, or exalt, races, classes, nationalities, or castes—"the rank is but the guinea's stamp, a man's a man for a' that." In its political aspects, democracy signifies government based on free discussion and uncoerced consent. Government is a means to an end; that end is the making available of the best conditions possible for the enjoyment, by all the governed, of life, liberty, and happiness. It follows that, so far as the democratic ideal is attained, men and women, without distinction of race, color, or creed, have the right to participate in government and to make of it an instrument that will minister to the needs of all. Equality of all citizens before the law is also an essential of a democratic social system. Democracy implies all these things, and the governments of free peoples today are working toward their full realization. Within recent years, however, the democratic concept has been vigorously challenged by the new Caesars of the authoritarian and totalitarian states. Individual liberty is derided, discipline and regimentation extolled; the State becomes all-important, the individual but a means to be used for the realization of state ends, and therefore to be bludgeoned and coerced into submission to the authority imposed from above. Freedom of press, assembly, and discussion—the way of democracy—is no longer tolerated. Ministers of propaganda and enlightenment are substituted to drug the public mind. Here lies the chief danger to peace in the world today. Entire populations are inoculated with the conviction that all their troubles arise from the fact that they have not had a fair deal in the world, that there is an unholy conspiracy to deprive them of the means of life. Therefore, they are told, it is necessary that they be made ready for war. Violence flourishes in the atmosphere of dictatorship, and dictators turn as naturally to threats and intimidation and violence for solutions in the field of foreign affairs as they have done for the solution of domestic problems. The democracies of the world are not threatening its peace today. They are supporters of the League of Nations, not because they are the satiated "haves" of the world, anxious to keep loot acquired in the past; the majority of them are "have nots" in the sense that they do not have great territories or great resources. But they do have the will-to-peace rather than the will-to-war, and it is as natural for them to look to the democratic methods of discussion and conciliation and respect for law as it is for the latter-day Caesars to flout law and disregard solemn obligations in the hot pursuit of power and prestige. Such ends, apparently, hallow all means. The methods of bluff and bluster are not the methods of peace, and he who proffers the world an olive branch that has "grown in a forest of 8,000,000 bayonets" is not seeking peace; he is inviting war.

I return to my earlier statement: Ultimately our peace and security, as well as the peace and security of others, must depend—it can *only* depend—upon the building up of a system of international law which will be respected by and applied to the strong as well as the weak. Of what value are more treaties if tomorrow they may be torn up as "scraps of paper" by governments who worship only at the altar of success and power? We do not need more treaties. We need more determination on the part of the democracies of the world to stand together against the continued violation of those that we already have. Within recent years the blood-and-iron statesmen have won their battles against law and decency in too great measure by default, because democratic statesmen have feared that any effective protest against the invasions of the rights of weak peoples and the contemptuous flouting of solemn commitments would precipitate war. These statesmen have relied upon reason and conciliation and, at the most, mild sanctions; and these have been of no avail because they did not go far enough. Such a policy may purchase peace for the current moment, but at a heavy price—the price of the continued crumbling of the structure of peace, and a guaranty of war tomorrow.

What should American policy be in the light of these developments? It would seem that we should give consistent and effective support to the present peace structure of the world by collaborating actively with the other democracies that are attempting to build up a system of collective security for great and small alike. The Kellogg Pact is insufficient for that purpose, for the reasons already stated. If peace is to be preserved, exhortation is not enough, good will is not enough, even the force of good example is not enough, and certainly a negative policy of isolated neutrality is not enough. Our neutrality legislation reflects the laudable purpose of trying to keep the country out of war, but it is certainly ill conceived as a means of helping to keep war out of the world; ill conceived because it treats aggressor and victim alike by pledging the country to aid neither. If tomorrow, for example, the Covenant of the League of Nations is again violated, and the Kellogg Pact, of which we are a signatory, is flouted by a wanton act of armed aggression against another signatory, we will merely call the matter to the attention of both the aggressor and the victim, remind both of them, with fine impartiality, of their obligations, and cut off war supplies to both parties. If the victim, as is likely to be true, is less well supplied with arms and war materials than the attacker, the policy actually works to the advantage of the aggressor. Moreover, if the League of Nations attempts to restrain the aggressor by the use of armed force, it, too, though in such an occurrence the defender of international law and the sanctity of treaties, can expect no aid from the United States. To me there is something a little ignoble in this attitude; but in any event we should not delude ourselves into thinking that it contributes to the prevention of war. Prospective lawbreakers are doubtless taking note, with a feeling of satisfaction, that when they are ready to march they can count on the disinterestedness of the United States.

This scuttle-to-cover policy of negativism must be abandoned if we care to be an effective force for peace and justice in the world. This does not mean that we should depart from the policy of "no entangling alliances"; that policy was sound in the days of Jefferson, and it is still sound. But it does mean that we should associate ourselves with the other nations that are struggling against great odds to stem the tide of a new series of barbarian invasions against the peace and security of peoples, and that are trying to make of the League of Nations and the World Court institutions capable of serving those peoples of the world who hate war and who want to lay the foundations of peace and security for their children. The League, it goes without saying, is not a perfect instrument, but it must be remembered that, together with its associated institutions, it has been the single forum of appeal and, however inadequate, the most effective force against international injustice and aggression since the World War. Moreover, recent obituary notices concerning it are, in my judgment, premature. But if there is something better calculated to do what the League has been trying to do, and what must be done if peace and security are to be measurably realized in our generation, then we should set about the task of its discovery and utilization. In any event the world must be organized against war and international tyranny. And whatever international authority is chosen as the agent of the community of civilized states, it must be endowed with power to see that the law of the community is obeyed by the strong as well as the weak, and that treaties are recognized as binding engagements rather than scraps of paper. Finally, the United States, in its own interests as well as in the interests of the civilization of which it inescapably forms a part, should play a vigorous, positive rôle consistent with the democratic ideals for which it stands, and commensurate with the position of power and influence which it enjoys.